LUMINAR 4
STEP BY STEP
THE PHOTOGRAPHER'S GUIDE TO LEARNING LUMINAR

By Nicole S. Young

LUMINAR 4: STEP BY STEP

The Photographer's Guide to Learning Luminar

Nicole S. Young

Published by Nicolesy®, Inc.
www.nicolesy.com

Copyright © 2020 Nicole S. Young, All Rights Reserved

Copy editor: Linda Laflamme
Indexed by: Valerie Haynes Perry
Layout, Design, and Photography: Nicole S. Young

NOTICE OF RIGHTS

All rights reserved. No part of this book may be reproduced, stored in a retrieval system, or transmitted in any form or by any means without the prior written permission of the publisher, except in the case of brief quotations embodied in critical articles or reviews.

LIABILITY

The information in this book is distributed on an "As-Is" basis, without warranty. Neither the author, the publisher, nor the companies owned by the author shall have any liability to any person or entity with respect to any loss or damage caused by or alleged to be caused directly or indirectly by the instruction contained in this book or by the websites or products described in it.

TRADEMARKS

Many of the designations used by manufacturers and sellers to distinguish their products are claimed as trademarks. Where those designations appear in this book, and Nicolesy®, Inc. was aware of a trademark claim, the designations appear as requested by the owner of the trademark. All other product names and services identified throughout this book are used in editorial fashion only and for the benefit of such companies with no intention or infringement of the trademark. No such use, or the use of any trade name, is intended to convey endorsement or other affiliation with this book. Adobe® Photoshop® is a registered trademark of Adobe Systems Incorporated in the United States and/or other countries. THIS BOOK IS NOT AUTHORIZED, ENDORSED OR SPONSORED BY ADOBE SYSTEMS INCORPORATED, PUBLISHER OF ADOBE® PHOTOSHOP®.

ISBN-13: 978-1-7323261-3-2
ISBN-10: 1-7323261-3-4

www.nicolesy.com

GETTING STARTED	**1**
DIGITAL DOWNLOADS	**7**

TOOLS & TECH

THE USER INTERFACE — 8
An introduction to Luminar 4

- The Luminar 4 Workspace • 10
- Top Toolbar • 12
- Library • 16
- Edit • 18
- Info • 23
- Looks • 24

MASTERING YOUR WORKSPACE — 26
Getting the most out of Luminar 4

- Setting Up the Workspace • 28
- Working with Files • 32
- Layers • 42
- Masking • 52
- Tools • 64
- Looks • 76
- Export and Batch Process • 81
- Luminar & Plug-ins • 85

ADJUSTMENT TOOLS — 90
Post-processing tools in Luminar 4

- Essentials • 92
- Creative • 105

A boat in Lofoten, Norway • Canon 6D, 70–200mm lens, 1/350 sec at f/11, ISO 100

TABLE OF CONTENTS

Portrait • 126

Professional • 130

START TO FINISH

HONEY BEE — **136**
A clean and colorful edit

ROCKY COAST — **150**
Bringing life to a gloomy sky

MOSSY FOREST — **168**
Processing a smartphone photograph

COOLING TOWER — **182**
Adding a new sky with style

SUNSET SILHOUETTE — **198**
Creating a composite with blend modes

FASHION PORTRAIT — **216**
Stylizing a portrait with Luminar

STARRY SKY — **230**
Transforming a photo from day to night

CONCLUSION — **247**

KEYBOARD SHORTCUTS — **248**

INDEX — **252**

A dew-covered dahlia • Canon 6D, 100mm macro lens, 1/125 sec at f/5.6, ISO 400

GETTING STARTED

Luminar 4 is a powerful photography application that is a good fit for both professionals and hobbyists alike. I find myself using Luminar's unique features regularly with my own photographs. It's a great program to use when I want to benefit from using easy-to-apply tools and Looks while still maintaining the integrity of my own personal post-processing style. Whether you want to process a photograph from start to finish, or polish an image previously edited within another photography application, I think you'll find Luminar to be a wonderful complement to your photographic endeavors.

WHAT IS LUMINAR?

Developed by Skylum Software, Luminar is an approachable and easy-to-use—yet extremely powerful—photography post-processing application. In it you can organize your images within a catalog, process raw photos,

Mossy trees on a log • iPhone 11 Pro, 1/40 sec at f/2.0, ISO 200

add basic and stylistic enhancements, mask, crop, work with layers, and so much more.

Some photographers will choose to use Luminar as their sole photography editing platform and will create a catalog referencing all of their image files. Others will use it as a plug-in, where they do their main editing in one application—such as Adobe® Lightroom® or Photoshop®—and then stylize the photograph by adding finishing touches inside of Luminar. It's a fantastic program with a lot of options and is a great addition to any photographer's toolbox.

WHAT'S NEW IN LUMINAR 4?

This version of Luminar added several new features and upgrades. Here are some of the standout updates and additions to Luminar 4:

- **Improved Interface:** The interface has changed with this version, separating the tools in four categories: Essential, Creative, Portrait, and Professional. Also, the Layers and Canvas panels have been organized into their own areas as well, allowing for a minimalistic and clutter-free workspace.

- **AI Sky Replacement:** One of the most impressive additions is the AI Sky Replacement tool. In a matter of seconds you can give your photo new life by adding a brand-new sky. There are several

Strawberries at a farmer's market • FUJIFILM X-T2, 18–55mm lens, 1/120 sec at f/2.8, ISO 200

default skies to choose from, and you can also add your own custom sky to a photograph as well.

- **Libraries**: The catalog in Luminar 4 makes it easy to use the program, even if you don't use Luminar as your only post-processing program. Plus, when working in the standalone program you also gain the advantage of non-destructive editing, where all changes are saved within the catalog and not directly applied to the image. This allows you to easily make changes to previously-edited files.

- **Portrait**: New tools have been added to Luminar, including AI face detection and the ability to quickly process photos of people. The software recognizes faces—even when there is more than one in an image—and applies portrait enhancements to only those areas.

WHO IS THIS BOOK FOR, AND WHAT WILL I LEARN?

This book is for photographers of all levels who would like to learn how to use Luminar 4 in their workflow, and it is particularly adapted for someone who wants to get a deep understanding of—as well as hands-on practice—using this program.

In this book, I explain each of the tools in the software, as well as demonstrate the *why* and *how* of processing several different types of images using start-to-finish examples. At the end of the book, you will have a solid grasp on how to use nearly all of the Luminar features and tools, along with some ideas on how to use the software to process your own photographs.

A tiny mushroom • FUJIFILM X-T3, 60mm macro lens, 1/60 sec at f/2.8, ISO 200

DIGITAL DOWNLOADS

PRACTICE IMAGES & VIDEO TUTORIALS

The tutorials in this book include free practice files that you can use to follow along with the step-by-step instructions throughout this book, as well as bonus videos with additional start-to-finish tutorials. Please use the link below to access this free download:

https://nicolesyblog.com/luminar-4-sbs

EBOOK FORMAT

This book also comes in eBook format (sold separately). Please use the link below for more information on this digital product:

https://store.nicolesy.com/products/luminar-4-step-by-step

A cosmos flower with texture added • FUJIFILM X-T3, 60mm macro lens, 1/1000 sec at f/2.8, ISO 160

Chapter 1

THE USER INTERFACE

An introduction to Luminar 4

Before I dive into post-processing, I would first like to familiarize you with the workspace you will be using to edit your photographs. This chapter is meant as a quick guide that will introduce you to the most-important panels and tools, as well as present this information in an easy-to-read reference. Think of this chapter as learning *what* each of the areas in the workspace are. To get more details on *how* to use the most important sections, please turn to *Chapter 2: Mastering Your Workspace*.

Feel free to flip back to this chapter if you need a reminder on a tool or section as you make your way throughout the processing steps within this book.

A fly on an echinacea flower • FUJIFILM X-T3, 60mm macro lens, 1/1000 sec at f/2.8, ISO 160

THE LUMINAR 4 WORKSPACE

A **Open:** Add a folder to the catalog, or open a single image to edit.

B **Looks Panel toggle:** Toggles the Looks panel at the bottom of the window.

C **Magnification:** Set the zoom level of the preview image.

D **Zoom Out/Zoom In:** Decrease or increase the magnification zoom level.

E **Quick Preview:** Toggles the before and after previews of your image.

F **Compare:** Adds a vertical split preview of the before-and-after image comparison.

G **Crop tool:** Crop, rotate, flip, and straighten a photo.

H **Share Image:** Export your photo to share or edit in another application.

I **Gallery images mode:** View all images from a folder/album as thumbnails.

J **Single image mode:** View a single image in the preview area.

K **Layout buttons:** Change the layout of your window (Library, Edit, and Info views).

L **Histogram:** The image's graphical representation of the color and tone values.

M **Layers:** View the Layers panel.

N **Canvas Tools:** Crop & Rotate, Erase, Clone & Stamp, and Lens & Geometry.

O **Tools area:** All active tools, depending on which option is selected on the right.

P **Image Adjustment Tools:** Essentials, Creative, Portrait, and Professional.

Q **History:** Displays a chronological list of each step taken in the application. Allows you to go back in time or reset your progress.

R **Menu pop-up:** Additional actions you can take with your photo (reset, copy settings, etc.)

S **Filmstrip:** A vertical display of all photos from the active folder or album.

T **Looks panel:** A list of all Looks within the selected category.

U **Looks Categories:** Shows a list of all available Looks categories.

V **Current photo actions:** Allows you to rate, favorite, label, and even delete the current photo.

W **Save New Look:** Save your own Look (saves to the User Luminar Looks category).

CHAPTER 1: THE USER INTERFACE

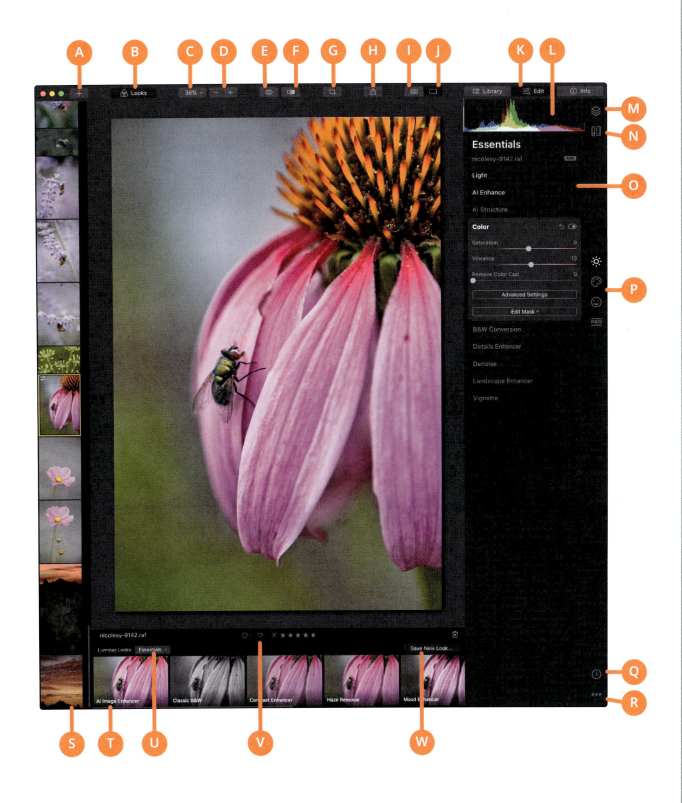

TOP TOOLBAR

The Top Toolbar is where you will find many of the functional commands that will be used regularly throughout your editing. Here you will find options for opening images, previewing your before and after states, as well as controls for panel visibility and other tools.

OPEN

The Open button allows you to add a folder of images to the Luminar library or edit a single image without adding it to the library. Click once on this button to open a drop-down menu where you can choose from these two options. When you select **Add Folder with Images** you are not moving folders into Luminar. Instead, Luminar is referencing them and allowing you quick access to their files from within the application.

LOOKS

The Looks button toggles the Looks (also referred to as "presets") filmstrip at the bottom of the window. This is where you will access and apply any **Luminar Looks** you have installed in the program. There is also a good selection of default Looks that are built in to the program you can use as well.

MAGNIFICATION

The Magnification buttons allow you to change the size of the image(s) you are previewing in the window. When you are in single image mode (one image viewed full-size in the window) then you have the option of setting the zoom level using either the percentage drop-down menu or with the Zoom Out and Zoom In buttons.

In **Gallery** view—when you see several thumbnails of your images within a folder or album in the preview area—the drop-down menu changes, allowing you instead to set the size of the thumbnails.

COMPARISON BUTTONS

The Comparison buttons are useful when previewing a photograph with edits applied. The **Quick Preview** button allows you to toggle the full before-and-after preview. Simply click and hold this button to see the comparison. You can also access the before-and-after preview quickly by pressing the **/** key on your keyboard.

The **Compare** button gives you a split-screen view of your image, with the *before* preview on the left and the *after* preview on the right. You can also move the separation line to the left or right to see how your edits affect different parts of the image. And if you would like to quickly toggle this preview on and off, you can do so with the **;** keyboard shortcut.

CROP TOOL

As with most photography software applications, Luminar allows you to crop your images with the Crop tool in the Top Toolbar. Activating this tool reveals a second toolbar with options to set your crop according to your preferences, such as the **Aspect** ratio, **Angle** (for straightening the horizon), two **Grid Overlays** to help with your composition, and the ability to **Flip** or **Rotate** the image.

SHARE IMAGE

When you are finished editing a photo, you will likely want to share it, and that's where the Share button comes into play. Clicking this button brings up a drop-down menu with options to export the photo, send it to a service or website, or even another application. The options you see in this menu may vary depending on the applications you have installed on your computer, as well as your operating system.

MODE SELECT

There are two Modes to choose from in Luminar: **Gallery images mode** and **Single image mode**. In *Gallery* view you will see all images as thumbnails from whichever folder or album is currently selected (if any) and *Single* mode will show you only the image that is active. You can also quickly toggle back and forth between these modes by pressing the **SPACEBAR**.

LAYOUT

Last in the toolbar are the Layout buttons. These buttons each toggle a different view in the right sidebar, each of which will be explained in depth in the next few pages:

- **Library**: This is where you view the folders and albums saved to your Luminar catalog. Here you can access and edit the photos you will quickly access inside of the application.

- **Edit**: Once you have a photo selected, you will activate the Edit layout to access all tools and layers to edit and stylize your photos.

- **Info**: The Info layout will show you detailed information about the selected image, including the histogram, file size, and metadata (date, camera, exposure settings, etc.).

LIBRARY

The Library view is where you can organize and access the photographs you have added to the catalog. You can also quickly access any single image edits you have made on images that are not in the catalog.

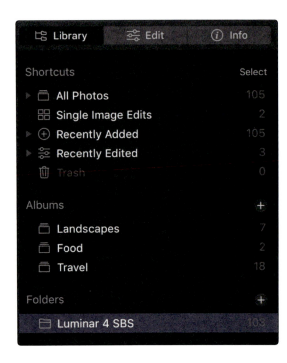

To access this view, click once on Library in the Layout section on the top-right of the window. Here you will see three categories: **Shortcuts**, **Albums**, and **Folders**. If you would like to hide one (or all) of these categories, simply hover over the name until you see Hide appear, then click. To reveal the category, hover over the name again until Show appears, then click and the category's contents will re-appear.

SHORTCUTS

The Shortcuts area is where you can view all of your images, or recently added and edited photos. It's an easy way to quickly access photos you have been working on or want to revisit. Clicking the **Select** button will

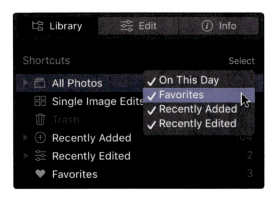

bring up a drop-down menu that you can use to filter the types of items displayed, allowing you to choose which you would like visible.

ALBUMS

Albums in Luminar allow you to organize your images into different categories, separate from where they are stored within the folders. Adding a photo to an album does not change the file's location on your computer. Instead, the album simply references the file, enabling you to add another layer of organization to your photographs.

Some ideas for albums might be photographic genres (landscapes, architecture, etc.), events (birthdays, vacations, etc.), collections for photo albums and prints, and so on. To create an album, click the ⊕ icon and give it a name. Any photos that are currently selected in your catalog will automatically be added, and you can also drag/drop photos from the Gallery images mode into the album as well.

FOLDERS

The Folders section is where you can reference folders and subfolders from your computer to quickly access them in Luminar. Adding a folder to the Luminar 4 catalog does not relocate the folder or files, but instead allows you to organize your images wherever you like on your computer. However, actions such as moving or deleting a photograph from Luminar will also move or delete it from its original folder.

EDIT

The Edit view is where the magic happens. Here you can apply stylizations to individual layers using tools (previously referred to as "filters"), as well as crop, rotate, and clone, stamp, and erase areas of the image as well.

LAYERS

The Layers button toggles the Layers panel where you can organize, re-arrange, add, delete, blend, mask, and transform layers in your file. If you are working on a single Image layer and applying only basic edits to your image, you may never need to access this section of Luminar. However, when you want to stack edits, mask a layer, or do composite work, then it's worth getting to know the features in the Layers panel.

One of the first things you'll notice is the small plus button ⊕ to the right of the panel. Clicking this brings up a small pop-up with three options:

- **Add New Adjustment Layer**: This adds an Adjustment layer where all of the stylization tools are reset, allowing you to stack other tools onto the base image. For example, if you wanted to add two Texture Overlay tools with two different textures, you would need to add another Adjustment layer and then apply the second texture in that new Adjustment layer. This is also a good technique to use when you want to apply a saved Look but also apply your own edits.

- **Add New Image Layer**: If you want to add a layer to do composite work, masking, or anything that requires layering, this is where you will select and add your new image from your computer.

- **Create New Stamped Layer**: When working on layers and applying stylized edits, adding a tool (such as a color enhancement, for example) applies that edit to the active layer only. However, if you have created a composite or added layers manually in the Layers panel, you may wish to apply global edits across all layers at once. In this situation you will first need to create a Stamped layer, which will collect all visible layers, create a new layer, and place it at the top of the Layers panel. Then you can stylize that layer as you wish so that all edits are applied to all elements of your visible image.

Another section of the Layers panel that you may want to familiarize yourself with is the individual layer options. This will be visible once you've added a layer (you will not see this when you only have a single layer active in your document).

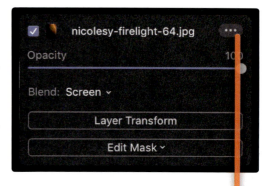

Clicking on the three dots to the right of the filename will bring up a menu with options for the layer itself, such as deleting, rasterizing, duplicating, etc. You can also set the **Blend** mode from this menu (although it is much easier to do within the layer itself), change the **Image Mapping** (which sets how the image is stretched and displayed on the canvas), and even control some of the **Mask** settings.

There are a few additional settings within this panel that allow you to blend, transform, and mask your layer:

- **Blend**: This is where you change the blending mode of the layer.

- **Layer Transform**: This option allows you to resize, flip, rotate, and relocate the layer within the document.

- **Edit Mask**: Here is where you can add a mask to your image (Brush, Radial, Gradient, or Luminosity).

CANVAS

The Canvas button reveals tools that allow you to alter the active layer. To make it easy to know which layer you are working on, the name of the layer is listed at the top of this panel.

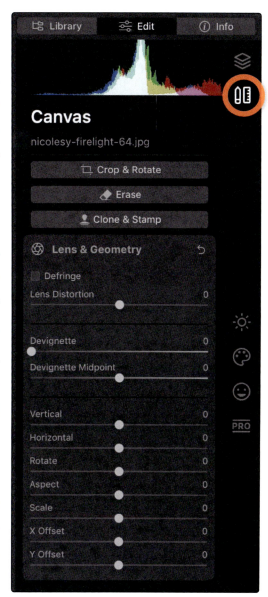

- **Crop & Rotate**: This tool is specifically for when you want to change the crop or rotation of the layer. It will affect only the active layer that you are currently working on. (To adjust the crop and rotation of the entire image, instead you will want to use the button in the Top Toolbar.)

- **Erase**: The Erase button allows you to erase sections of your photograph. It's best for minor blemishes and small spots.

- **Clone & Stamp**: Using the Clone & Stamp feature is best for larger areas you want to remove and have more control over.

- **Lens & Geometry**: If your photograph has lens distortion, or fringing along the edges, then this is the section you will want to use to help correct it.

IMAGE ADJUSTMENTS

The main Image Adjustments section in the Edit view contains all of the stylization adjustments you can add to your photograph and will very likely be your most-frequented area of Luminar. The tools in this area are separated into four categories, but don't read into the categories too much. Once you start working with Luminar you'll quickly learn your "go-to" tools, regardless of the group they live in.

- **Essentials**: This group contains many of the most common tools, such as Light, AI™ Enhance, AI Structure, B&W Conversion, and more. You'll want to start here with your edits to create a "clean slate" before moving on to the more creative tools.

- **Creative**: Here you will find some of the more stylistic tools, such as the new AI Sky Replacement, Color Styles (LUT), Texture Overlays, and so on.

- **Portrait**: If you have people in your photos, then this will be a helpful group of tools for you to use as it encompasses many of the tools that are commonly used with portraits. However, some tools, such as the Orton Effect, look wonderful on many other genres of images as well.

- **Professional**: The remaining tool group allows you to add even more color and contrast to your photographs, one of my favorites being the **Dodge & Burn** tool (which lets you selectively lighten and darken areas of your image). The tools in this group are powerful and can add an extra element of intrigue and beauty to your images.

INFO

The Info view shows you the metadata details about your image, including the image's name, file size, date, camera, lens, exposure, and so on. This, along with the Edit view, also shows the image's histogram at the top. In the standard mode you will view the full-spectrum of the histogram, but if you would like to isolate a specific color to see what it looks like, simply click once in the histogram area to toggle the red, green, blue, and tonal values.

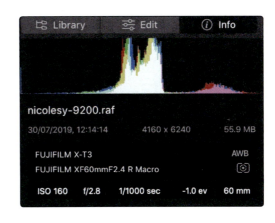

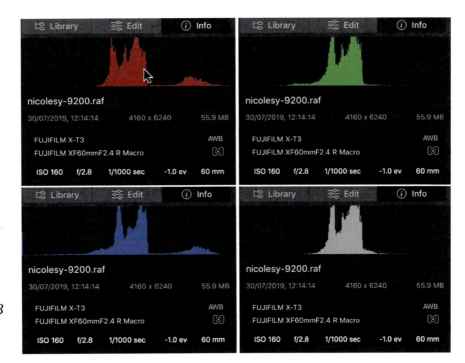

By clicking the histogram area you can toggle the RGB values of your photograph.

LOOKS

The Looks panel, located in the filmstrip at the bottom of the window, can be toggled on and off by pressing the **Looks** button near the top of the application. By default your version will come pre-installed with a small selection of Looks you can work with. And it's also possible that you've downloaded and installed third-party packs as well.

This is my current collection of Luminar Looks. The default Looks are at the top, and I've also created several packs of my own.

To apply a Look, first choose a category using the Luminar Looks category selector. Then, click the pack you want to work with, and each Look will show a preview of itself applied to your image within the bottom filmstrip. Clicking a Look will apply the effects to your image, but keep in mind that it will also remove any existing edits you've added. It's often a good idea to first add a new *Adjustment layer* using the Layers panel so that you can stack a Look on top of your original edits.

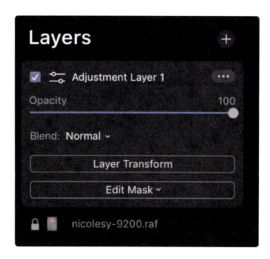

Another thing you can do is save your own Look that you can apply to other images. Once you have finished editing a photo, click the Save New Look button and give your Look a name. (Note that the Look will only save stylization tools only on the currently-active layer.) This new Look will then be saved to the *User Luminar Looks* category.

RESET ADJUSTMENTS

If you would like to reset all settings for an image and start over, the best way to do this is to access the menu pop-up in the lower-right corner of the application while in the Edit view. Click the menu and select Reset Adjustments at the top to bring your photo back to its original settings.

Chapter 2

MASTERING YOUR WORKSPACE

Getting the most out of Luminar 4

In the previous chapter, I discussed *what* each of the panels and items are within the Luminar workspace. In this chapter, I will get into detail on *how* you can use those features with your own photography workflow, as well as describe some of the important uses and applications of many of the tools.

A fiddlehead fern in Oregon • FUJIFILM X-T3, 60mm macro lens, 1/140 sec at f/2.4, ISO 160

SETTING UP THE WORKSPACE

When you open up Luminar 4 for the first time, the workspace viewing area will be at a default setting. For the most part, you may be happy with this setup and never feel the need to customize. But there may be times when you want to view things a little differently. In this section, I'll show you how you can work with the settings within Luminar to view your workspace in a way that suits your needs.

PANEL & SIDEBAR VISIBILITY

One thing you may want to play with is the visibility of the panels. If you find that you are not using a certain panel, toolbar, or sidebar, you may want to hide it to keep your workspace tidy and more minimalistic, allowing you to focus on the task at hand. Here are some ways you can go about customizing what you in the application:

- **All panel visibility**: To quickly hide the panels and see the image only, press the **TAB** key. This will hide the left filmstrip, right sidebar, and the Looks panel at the bottom. (The toolbar at the top will remain visible.)

- **Individual panel visibility**: If you want to hide specific panels only, you can do so from the menu at the top. Go to the **View** option in the menu bar, and select from the three **Hide/Show** options.

- **Full-screen (Mac only):** If you would like to toggle the application in or out of full-screen mode, press the **F** key. When in full-screen mode, only the Luminar application will be visible, allowing you to keep your desktop tidy and focus on your edits.

BACKGROUND COLOR

Another thing you may want to do is set the background color of the application to a different shade, ranging from very dark to white. The color of the background can sometimes help with your editing, depending on the final destination of your image. For example, if you know that your photo will be framed with a white mat surrounding the image, you may want to preview the image with a white background in the application to give you a better feel for how the final print will look.

There are a few different ways to access this command. First, you can go into the menu at the top and choose **View > Background Color**. However, a much easier method is to right-click the background; all of the color options will pop up.

RAW + JPEG PAIRS

Many cameras have the ability to photograph images in both raw and JPEG at the same time. However, when adding these files to a catalog it can give the appearance of having duplicate images. When editing files on the computer you will most likely want to work with the raw version of the file, and the Luminar 4 application allows you to choose which version is visible (raw, JPEG, or both) so that you are viewing and working with the image version you want only. Keep in mind that this setting affects the *visibility* of the files, and not whether or not they are still located in your folder and catalog.

To access this setting, go to **View > Raw + JPEG Pairs** and select the type of images you want visible. I recommend choosing the **Show Raw Only** option so that you are getting the most out of your file and editing the best version possible.

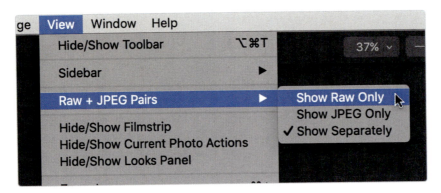

PREVIEW CLIPPING

One thing that is good practice for photographers is to be aware of the amount of white and black clipping in a photograph. Clipping is when the whites or blacks are pure white or pure black, which is typically not ideal with most photographs. An area that is pure white or black means that it has lost all shadows and details, which are probably something you will want to maintain. There are exceptions to this, such as when you want a pure white or black background, but for the most part you will want to reduce the amount of clipping in your photograph as much as possible.

To preview the clipped areas, you can go to **View** > **Hide/Show Clipping**, but a faster way is to press the **J** key on your keyboard. When you do this, any clipped areas in your photo they will show up as red (white clipped areas) or blue (black clipped areas).

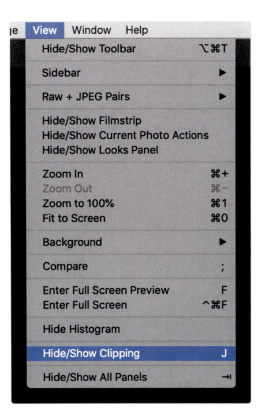

This image shows both white and black clipped areas, indicated by the bright red and blue in the photograph.

WORKING WITH FILES

Luminar 4 supports a wide variety of graphic formats, including JPEG, PNG, TIFF, and PSD (Mac only). It also supports most raw formats, and they are updating it regularly to keep it up-to-date with current camera models. However, if you are working with a raw format with a camera that is not supported, one workaround is to use the [Adobe DNG converter](), which converts raw files into DNGs. These are still raw files but in a file type that works with applications that do not yet support certain camera models.

When using Luminar 4, you can organize your photo library in the Luminar catalog, or you can edit single files and still use your existing file organization method. This flexibility makes Luminar 4 widely adaptable to your existing workflow.

UNDERSTANDING THE LUMINAR CATALOG

The catalog in Luminar is a reference to your images. When your photos are added to a catalog, the files still reside in your folder structure on your computer or hard drive. The catalog remembers where those files are located and gives you quick access to them. The act of adding files to the catalog does not relocate them on your computer.

When you apply edits to an image, these edits are saved within the catalog, and these in-progress edits can be viewed only inside of the Luminar application. The catalog does not store the original photos, but instead keeps a copy of the edits you have applied to those files.

CHAPTER 2: MASTERING YOUR WORKSPACE

One important thing that you may wish to do is back up the catalog to an external or cloud-based drive. Luminar creates regular backups of your catalog but because they are in the same location as your original catalog they are still at risk if something happens to your hard drive. It's best to have an additional "off-site" backup, so if anything bad happens to the hard drive where the main catalog is stored, you will not lose any of your Luminar edits.

MANUALLY BACKING UP THE CATALOG:

1. In Luminar, go to **File** > **Catalog** > **Show in Finder** (Windows users please use the **Show in Explorer** option).

2. Go up to the previous parent folder (this will be the name of your Luminar catalog). Select and copy this folder.

3. Access a back-up location on either an external/separate hard-drive, or a cloud-based drive, and paste the folder to this location. ■

If at any time you need to restore your backed-up catalog, you can simply copy the folder you backed up to your main computer, and then go to **File** > **Catalog** > **Open** and locate it. Also, Mac users can go to **File** > **Catalog** > **Restore from Backup** to restore a catalog as well.

To restore a backed-up catalog, go to File > Catalog > Open. Or, if on a Mac, you can use the Restore from Backup option.

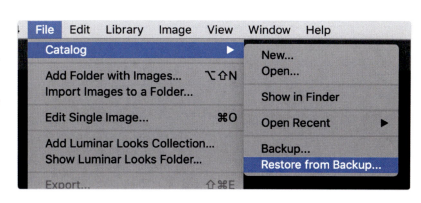

33

When you first open Luminar 4 it creates a new catalog by default. However, you can also have more than one catalog if you prefer. This is a great way to add an extra element of organization to your photos. For example, if you work with clients, you may want to maintain a separate catalog for each client to help stay better organized.

To create a new catalog, go to **File** > **Catalog** > **New**. Then, give your new catalog a name and make sure it is stored in the folder you would like (Luminar will likely open to the default location on your computer, which will typically be a good place to keep it). Then, add or import files to this new catalog to begin using it.

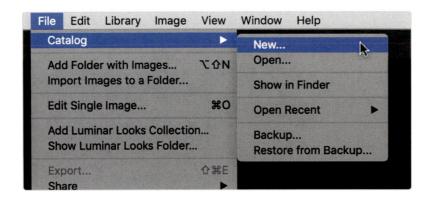

Note: All of your imported and user-created Looks are stored system-wide, so you will be able to access them from within any of your Luminar catalogs.

ADDING FILES TO THE CATALOG

Using Luminar 4 as the way to organize your images is very straightforward. First, you will need to have files that you have already imported to your computer or a memory card from which you wish to import your photos.

CHAPTER 2: MASTERING YOUR WORKSPACE

IMPORTING FROM A MEMORY CARD:

1. Connect your memory card to your computer.

2. In Luminar, navigate to the folder you wish to import your photos into. If you don't currently have a folder you want to use for the group of photos you are about to import, now is the time to create one. To do this, in the Library view (right sidebar), access the Folders section. Then, either click the ⊕ icon to add a new top-level folder, or you can right-click over an existing folder to create a new subfolder.

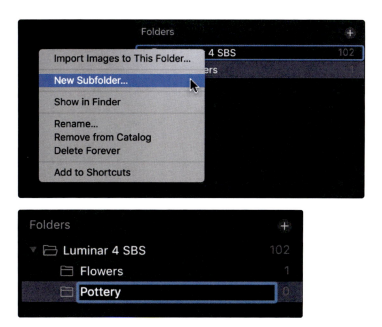

3. In the menu, go to **File > Import Images to a Folder**.

35

4. Navigate to your connected memory card, and locate the files you wish to import. You can either highlight individual files, or click Import to Folder to import all images on the memory card. ■

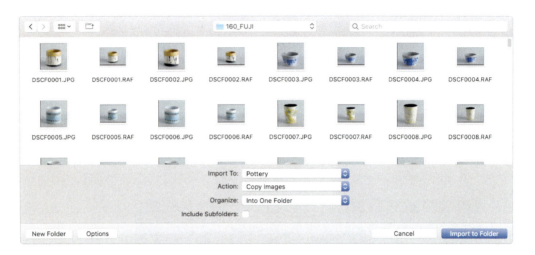

ADDING FILES FROM A FOLDER:

1. There are a handful of ways to initiate an import from an existing folder: In the menu bar, go to **File** > **Add Folder with Images**. Or, in the Library view on the right, click the ⊕ icon. You can also click the Open icon located on the top-left of the application window and choose **Add Folder with Images**.

2. Navigate to the folder of images you wish to add to the catalog, and click Add Folder. Your folder of images will now appear in the **Folders** section in the **Library** view in your Luminar 4 catalog. ■

CHAPTER 2: MASTERING YOUR WORKSPACE

Another thing you may want to do is move photos around, or even remove a folder of images from a catalog. Moving photos around is quite simple, and all it takes is dragging the photos from the grid view into a folder on the sidebar. (Keep in mind that this will also relocate the photos on your hard drive.)

You can also remove an entire folder of images from the catalog as well. To do this, right-click the folder you wish to remove and select Remove from Catalog. (This works at top-level folders only, not subfolders.) A confirmation window will pop up letting you know that the folder of images will be removed from the catalog only, but will still remain on your hard drive.

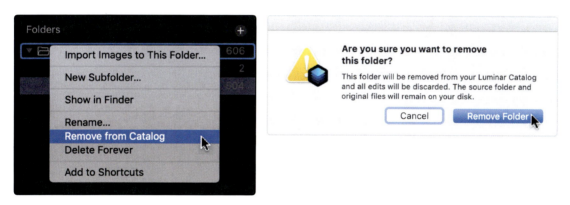

Alternately, if you wish to delete a folder of images, you can select the Delete Forever option. As the name suggests, this will permanently delete the folder and images. Please use this option with extreme caution!

PHOTO ACTIONS

Another way to organize your photos is to use ratings, color labels, and flags:

- **Ratings**: The ratings are on a scale of 0 to 5, and are visualized using stars.

- **Color Labels**: You can choose to either have no color label (default), or add a Red, Yellow, Green, Blue, or Purple label to your photo.

- **Flags**: There are two types of flags: **Flagged** and **Rejected**. A Flagged photo will have the *heart* filled-in, and a Rejected photo will have the *X* highlighted. You can also set a photo to be Unmarked, which is the default setting for all images that are imported or added to the catalog.

How you decide to use these photo actions—along with their meanings—will be completely up to you. I tend to favorite images that I like most (typically the best images from a given photo shoot) and also will add color labels to group photos depending on the project I am working on.

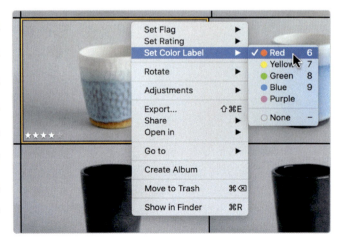

There are several ways that you can apply these actions to your images. First, you can right-click an image in any view to access a pop-up menu and apply whichever type of photo action you like. Also, in the Gallery

LUMINAR 4: STEP BY STEP

images mode (thumbnail grid view) there are small icons that appear as you hover over an image, allowing you to either rate or flag a photo.

You can also use keyboard shortcuts to go through a set of images and apply ratings and flags. I find that this is the best way to quickly cull a photo shoot to find and separate out the very best images. My preference is to use the arrow keys to step through each image, and when I find one I like, I press the **P** key, which fills in the heart and sets the image to *Flagged*. You can also reject images with the **X** key, or rate them and add color labels using the number keys (**0–5** will add ratings, and **6–9** will apply a color label).

Please view the Keyboard Shortcuts *section near the end of the book for a full list of all Luminar keyboard shortcuts.*

ALBUMS

When you want to group photos together from different folders, using albums is an ideal way to do this. Adding a photo to an album does not move the file, but rather creates a reference to the image inside of a "virtual" type of folder. Some uses for albums might be to group photos based on their type (landscapes, portraits, etc.), project-based images (such as a group of photos you want to print for a photo album or gallery showing), and so on.

CREATING AND USING ALBUMS:

1. To create an album, first make sure you are in the Library view. Then, highlight an image or a group of images that you want to initially add to the album.

2. In the right sidebar, click the ⊕ icon next to the **Albums** category. The photos you selected will automatically be added and you are able to give your new album a name.

3. To add more photos to the album, simply highlight them in the grid and drag them over to the album you want to place them in. ■

EDITING A SINGLE FILE

If you prefer not to use the Luminar 4 as your main image catalog, you can still make use of all of the editing features within the application. To do this, you will need to select your files one at a time. The good news is that the files are still "remembered"  in the Luminar catalog, even though the folder they are contained within is not actually added. At the top of the right sidebar is a Shortcuts section, and **Single Image Edits** is one of these categories. Each time you edit a single image it is "added" to this category for easy access down the road.

There are a few different ways that you can open a single image into Luminar 4. The first method is using the Open icon located on the top-left corner of the application. Clicking this will display a drop-down menu, and selecting **Edit Single Image** will bring up a window where you can navigate to the file you need.

You can also access this same option from the menu bar. Go to **File > Edit Single Image**, and a window will pop up to navigate to your file.

Once your image has opened, you can then go to the Edit view and use any of the tools to stylize your photo as you like. You can even rate and label your image, just like you would with any photo within the catalog.

LAYERS

You can easily edit a photo and add all of your filters to only one layer, but there may be times when this is not always the best option. Luminar allows you to work with multiple layers—either Image or Adjustment layers—and each of these layers can also be further enhanced with tools.

To begin, you can access the Layers panel by clicking the icon in the right sidebar.

LAYERS PANEL OVERVIEW

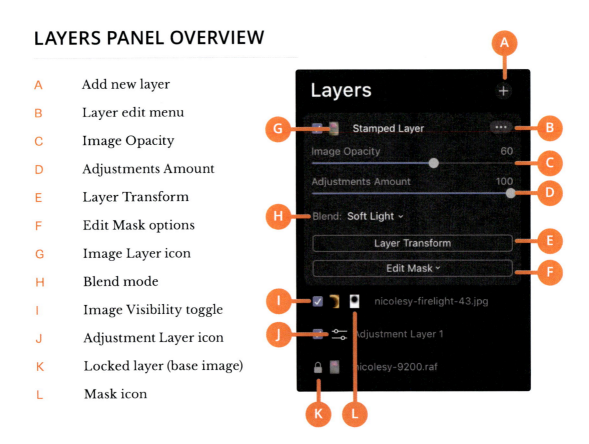

A	Add new layer
B	Layer edit menu
C	Image Opacity
D	Adjustments Amount
E	Layer Transform
F	Edit Mask options
G	Image Layer icon
H	Blend mode
I	Image Visibility toggle
J	Adjustment Layer icon
K	Locked layer (base image)
L	Mask icon

TYPES OF LAYERS

There are three main types of layers you can work with inside of Luminar: Adjustment, Image, and Stamped:

- **Image Layer**: An Image layer is a layer with some type of graphics file which, in most cases, is a photograph. You may want to use this option when manually adding a new sky, applying and blending an overlay, or creating a composite image.

- **Adjustment Layer**: Adding an Adjustment layer is a good way to stack Looks, blend tools, or just keep your edits separated. For example, maybe you are working on a portrait image and would prefer to keep the edits to the *face* separate from edits you may make to the *overall image*.

  Adjustment layers also allow you to cohesively combine composite layers together by adding overall adjustments to an entire image. I'll demonstrate how to do this in the *Start to Finish* section later on in the book.

- **Stamped Layer**: Creating a Stamped layer merges all of the *visible* layers in the Layers panel into one layer, and then places this new layer at the top of the Layers panel. This is another way to create an Image layer but by using the existing images and adjustments already within the Layers panel.

LAYERS OPTIONS

Within each layer you have additional options to work with:

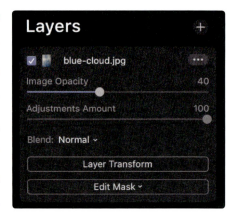

- **Image Opacity**: The Image Opacity setting allows you to change the opacity of the entire layer. This is helpful when you want to reduce the intensity of an adjustment, an image layer, or a combination of the two. In the example below, I added a new Image layer and wanted it to be slightly transparent, so I decreased the **Image Opacity** setting to **40%**.

In the above images, a Texture Overlay was added as a new layer and then the Image Opacity slider was reduce to 40%. This makes the texture image slightly transparent so that the image below can show through.

CHAPTER 2: MASTERING YOUR WORKSPACE

- **Adjustments Amount**: Whenever you add any new layer you are able to add adjustment tools to stylize the image. The Adjustments Amount slider will then let you reduce the amount of the effects you add, so moving this slider to the left will make the adjustments themselves more transparent. I tend to use this option when I add a *Look* and the effect is too intense, and reducing the **Adjustments Amount** slider allows me to create a more subtle outcome. In the example below, the first image shows the adjustments at 100%, but reducing the slider to 50% softens the effects.

Here the Adjustments Amount slider is at 100%.

Reducing the Adjustments Amount slider to 50% reduces the intensity of the effects.

- **Blend**: Blend modes allow you to change how a layer blends with the layers below. One common use of blending modes is when applying textures. You can also blend Adjustment layers, as shown in the example below. Playing with these settings can give a photograph an entirely different feel.

In this set of images, the photo starts out with no adjustments A *. Then, a simple black-and-white adjustment is added* B *and the layer's Blend mode is changed to Overlay* C *. Blending the layer with the photo gives it a unique look.*

LUMINAR 4: STEP BY STEP

- **Layer Transform**: The Layer Transform button will display a new menu at the top (just above the preview area) allowing you to flip, rotate, and resize the layer you are working on. This differs from the *Crop & Rotate* tool because it affects the active layer only, not the entire image canvas, and it only applies to Image layers.

When I add a new Image layer, by default it fills in and stretches to fit the aspect ratio of the original image D *. In this case, the original image is square (1:1 ratio), but the image I added is a standard 2:3 ratio. So I used Layer Transform to help "un-squish" the Image layer* E *and then blended it with the original image* F *.*

- **Edit Mask**: The Edit Mask menu allows you to add a new mask to your image. When you click it, you can choose between a *Brush*, *Radial*, *Gradient*, or *Luminosity Mask*. (Please turn to the *Masking* section in this chapter for more detailed information on adding a mask to your image.)

LAYER EDIT MENU

In addition to the options shown in an individual layer, there is also a drop-down menu to the right of each layer name that gives you more options to work with (click to access this menu). When you are working on the base (locked) layer, these options are limited. However, when you have either an **Image layer** or **Adjustment layer**, you will have more settings to work with.

- **Hide/Show Layer**: If you would like to hide the layer (or show a previously-hidden layer) then you can choose this option. Alternately, you can use the Image Visibility toggle to the left of the layer's name which is a much faster way to go back and forth. This setting is useful when you want to see how a specific layer affects your image without doing a full before-and-after preview.

- **Rasterize Layer**: Using the Rasterize Layer option "flattens" the layer by permanently applying any masks or adjustments added, and removes the ability to further edit those adjustments.

- **Duplicate Layer**: This setting allows you to duplicate any layer within the Layers panel.

- **Rename Layer**: Use this option if you would like to rename your layer. By default it will be either the image's filename or the type of layer ("Adjustment Layer" or "Stamped Layer"). Renaming layers is a great way to keep your workspace organized. In the example below, I renamed "Adjustment Layer 2" to read "B&W Conversion" so it was easier to understand which layer was doing what within the workspace.

- **Blend**: The Blend setting within the menu is another way to access the same Blend setting that you see within the Layers panel.

- **Image Mapping**: The Image Mapping feature is most helpful when adding images to the Layers panel. For example, if you are working on a vertical photograph but drop in a horizontal sky, by default Luminar will **Fill** the horizontal image to fit into the entire vertical image frame.

  It's more likely that you will want to change this option so that the image is not warped. **Scale to Fit** sets the image to its original aspect ratio, but also pushes a lot of the image off of the frame. The **Fit** option, on the other hand, retains the layer's original aspect ratio, but contains the image within the document's frame.

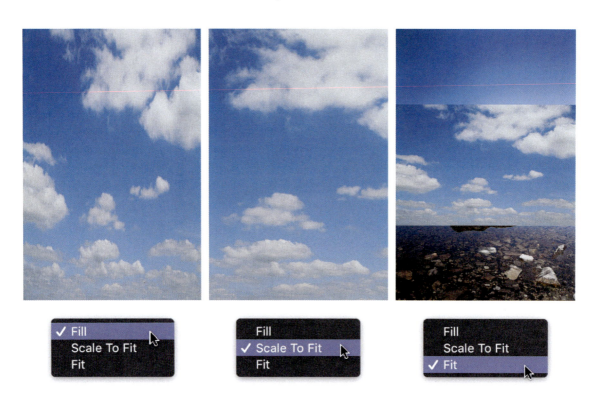

- **Mask**: The last option within the Layer Edit menu is the ability to edit a mask. (Please turn to the *Masking* section in this chapter for more detailed information on these settings.)

STACKING ADJUSTMENTS

If you work with Looks, the ability to stack Adjustment layers can be a huge benefit. Let's say you want to make some basic edits to a raw file, but also use a Look from another pack that has additional adjustments, all on the same image. Stacking different Looks and adjustments is the best way to do this, because adding a Look will overwrite your original adjustments. Doing this is as simple as adding a new Adjustment layer within the **Layers panel**. Then, any adjustments or Looks you add will only apply to that layer, but will be visible on your main image.

For this example, I first made some edits to the raw file G *(white balance, tone, etc.). I also wanted to add a bokeh overlay Look I have in my collection, but applying it after my initial adjustments would have erased those edits. So instead, I added a new Adjustment layer and then applied the Overlay Look to that layer* H *.*

MASKING

Masking is an important part of the photographer's workflow. With masking you can make selective adjustments, create composite images, and even replace a boring sky. Luminar's masking abilities, while straightforward, can be extremely powerful. Within this section I will discuss the tools and why you may want to apply them to your photographs.

WHAT IS MASKING?

Masking is ability to *hide* or *reveal* certain parts of a layer or adjustment without actually *deleting* any of the edits. It's a non-destructive and re-editable way to selectively adjust parts of a photograph, which is one reason it can be so powerful.

If you're new to masking—and maybe even a little intimidated by it—I'm here to help! The basics of masking are these two things: black and white. Any *black* area of a mask *hides* that layer, while any *white* area of the mask *reveals* what is on that layer, and you will see this represented within the mask on the Layers panel. Plus, any shade of gray on the mask applies a lower-opacity mask as well. Within Luminar, you can do this by brushing, adding a gradient, or even adding a Luminosity mask, which I will explain later on in this section.

Before I get into detail on the types of masks you can use in Luminar, let's look at a few examples of what a mask looks like after being added to an image. In this first example, I added a Texture Overlay, but only wanted the texture to appear in the background, so I needed to mask out the mushroom and foreground. The mask preview is represented by a red overlay, which shows the white areas within that layer that are visible.

Before

With Image layer and mask

After

In this next example, I added an Adjustment layer with a Color tool applied to alter the hue of the image, making it blue. Then, I masked the image so that one of the lanterns shows this difference in color.

Before

With Adjustment layer and mask

After

TYPES OF MASKS

Luminar has four different types of masks, each of which can be used independently or in combination with the others. You can access the masking options by clicking the Edit Mask drop-down menu within a layer on the Layers panel.

- **Brush**: Brushing is the most basic type of creating a mask. Using it is simple: You brush to either *hide* (**Erase**) or *reveal* (**Paint**) an area of a layer or filter.

    When active, the Brush tool has several options: **Size**, **Softness**, and **Opacity**. These can be accessed either from the top part of the window or by right-clicking the image. *Softness* determines how soft or hard the edge of the brush will be, and *Opacity* sets how opaque or translucent each brush stroke is as you sweep across.

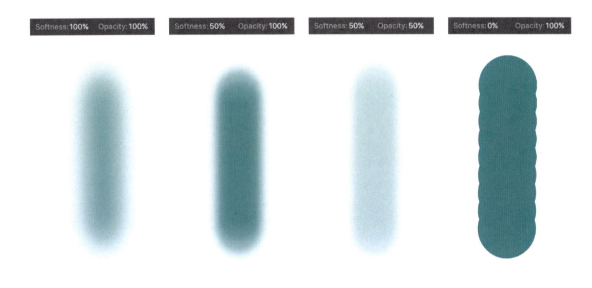

- **Radial Mask**: The Radial Mask option adds a round, feathered gradient mask to an image. This is a useful tool when you want to create a quick and subtle 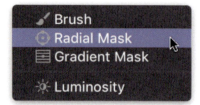 perfectly-round mask to one large area of an image to either hide or reveal an adjustment or layer.

In the example below, I added a new **Adjustment layer** and then used the Light tool to darken the image. Then, I applied a **Radial mask** to create a custom vignette so that the original image shows through in the center of the image, but the rest displays the adjustments added on the new layer.

Before

With adjustments added

Mask applied

After

- **Gradient Mask**: Gradient masks work well when you want to add a filter or layer effect to the top, bottom, left, or right portion of the image. Some examples 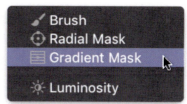 of using this mask are to darken a sky, lighten a foreground, or even blend together two images of the same scene photographed at different exposure settings.

In the example below I wanted to make the foreground brighter without affecting the sky. So I added a new **Adjustment layer** and then made some tonal edits to add brightness, and then applied a **Gradient mask**. This hides the sky area so that only the foreground is affected by the adjustments in that layer.

Before

With adjustments added

Mask applied

After

- **Luminosity Mask**: Lastly, Luminar has the ability to create **Luminosity masks**. These masks tend to enhance an image in a subtle way, but can be 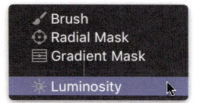 extremely useful. Luminosity masks create a mask that is based on the tonal values of the image. *Dark* areas are masked out (hidden), while *bright* areas remain visible. In Luminar, you are likely to use this tool for targeted adjustments to either the bright or dark areas of a photo.

Before *Mask applied* *After*

In the above example, I wanted to apply adjustments to *only* the dark areas of the image and keep the light beams untouched. So I added a **Luminosity mask** to an **Adjustment layer** and inverted it, so I could freely add my adjustments knowing that they would primarily affect only the darker areas of the image.

LAYER VS. ADJUSTMENT MASKING

There are two ways to mask in Luminar: You can either mask the entire layer or mask individual adjustments.

- **Layer Masking**: Masking an entire Image or Adjustment layer is ideal when you have an image or group of filters you want to mask all at once. You might use this option when blending two images together (replacing a background or sky), or when you want to make several edits and then selectively adjust a large area, such as intensifying the sky in a sunset photograph.

- **Adjustment Masking**: Each individual adjustment within the Tools panel can be masked on its own exactly as you would apply a mask in the Layers panel. This type of masking is ideal when you have one enhancement that you want to apply to only a portion of the image, such as masking a sharpening layer to affect only the eyes in a photograph while leaving all other adjustments as-is.

ADDITIONAL MASK CONTROLS

After applying a mask to a layer or filter, you can use the additional controls to further enhance the mask. The best way to access these settings is to first create a mask through either the layer or adjustment, and then use the Mask drop-down menu in the options that appear on the top-left area of the window. (If you already have an existing mask on a layer or adjustment, you can activate the **Brush** tool to get into the masking screen.)

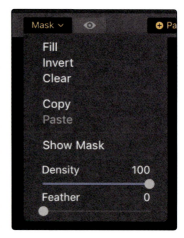

- **Fill**: This fills the mask with *white* and deletes any existing masking, *revealing* the contents on the layer or filter.

- **Invert**: This option *inverts* the existing mask.

- **Clear**: Using this fills the mask with *black* and deletes any existing masking, *hiding* the contents of the layer or filter.

- **Copy and Paste**: These are good options if you want to re-use a mask within a document. Luminar does not allow for copying and pasting *between* multiple open documents, however.

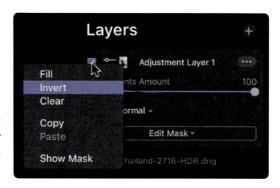

Several of these Mask Controls can also be accessed by right-clicking an existing mask within either the layer or adjustment.

- **Density**: Think of the Density setting as a *mask opacity* slider. At 100% the mask is fully opaque, but when you reduce the Density slider to a lower percentage, then the masked areas start to become see-through. In the example below, I added a **Texture Overlay** and then masked it with a Radial mask in order to subdue the texture effect on the flower. Then, using the **Mask Controls**, I set the **Density** to **50%** to allow some of the texture to show through.

Before

Texture and mask applied

Mask Density at 50%

By setting the Density of the mask to 50%, the watercolor Texture Overlay begins to show through the mask area, allowing a subtle amount of the texture to appear on the masked flower area.

- **Feather**: The Feather setting helps soften the edges of a mask. Use this when you want to further blend the transition between the masked and unmasked areas of an image. In the example below, I first applied a Luminosity mask to an Adjustment layer (the mask preview is currently active in this image as indicated by the red overlay).  Then, using the Mask Controls, I increased the **Feather** setting to blur the harsh edges of the mask.

Mask Feather set to 0

Mask Feather set to 87

- **Show and Hide a Mask**: Sometimes you may want to temporarily disable—or hide—a mask. You can do this by selecting the Hide Mask option from any Mask drop-down menu, or a quicker way is to press the SHIFT key and then click the mask in either the Layers panel or on the adjustment tool it is applied to. When a mask is hidden it will have a red X over it. Repeat these steps to enable the mask by selecting Show Mask in the Mask drop-down menu or using the Shift-click shortcut method.

- **Previewing the Mask**: You may also want to preview the mask you are making, or have already created, to ensure that you have masked only the areas you want. To do this, first make sure that you have one of the masking tools active. Then, click the eyeball icon 👁 in the options at the top. (Alternately, you can use the **/** key to toggle the mask preview visibility.) This will show you a red preview of the mask. The red color represents the *visible* areas of the mask (whatever is on the layer or adjustment will be visible), and anything that is see-through will hide that portion of the layer.

One thing to keep in mind is that some of the masking controls are visible only when the **Brush** tool is active, but all settings can be applied to any *previously-created* mask. For example, let's say you apply a Gradient mask but want to reduce its density, but you can't find this setting in the options in the top-left while you are still applying the Gradient mask. In order to view these additional controls, first finish applying the Gradient mask. Then, on the same layer or adjustment you are working on, activate the Brush tool. The "missing" options are now visible, and you can adjust the mask you just created using the Density tool or any other setting you see in the list.

TOOLS

All of the tools in Luminar 4 are located on the right sidebar. These tools are separated into two main categories: **Canvas Tools** and **Image Adjustments**. The Canvas tools are all located within the Canvas button, located just below the Layers button, while the Image Adjustments are broken down into four categories and are centrally located within the right sidebar.

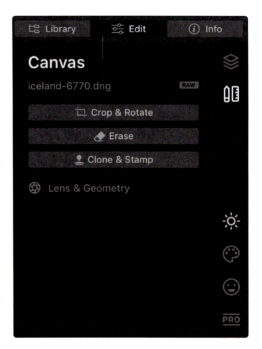

CROP & ROTATE

The Crop & Rotate tool allows you to crop, resize, rotate, and flip the document (vertically or horizontally). After activating the Crop tool you will see the following options at the top of the window:

- **Aspect**: The Aspect setting lets you choose a specific aspect ratio for your image, such as **1:1**, **2:3**, or **4:5**. By default Aspect is set to **Free**, which allows you to crop the image into any aspect ratio you like. However, if you're like me and prefer to stick to standard aspect ratios, then you will either want to choose a setting from the list or—better yet—click the lock icon 🔒 to keep the aspect ratio the same as your image was originally set to.

CHAPTER 2: MASTERING YOUR WORKSPACE

- **Angle**: This setting allows you to rotate the image at a specific angle by using a slider that appears when you click on the setting **I**. However, I find that this method is a bit tedious and prefer to rotate within the image view itself. I do this by first hovering over one of the corners of the crop area, and then I click and drag once the small rotate rounded line with two arrows appears **J**.

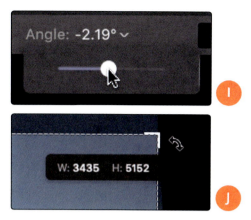

- **Grid View**: The two grid-like buttons will let you preview the image with two different overlays. They don't affect the overall cropping of your photo but can help guide you to achieve a better composition.

- **Flip and Rotate**: There are three icons that allow you to flip and rotate the image: **Flip Vertically**, **Flip Horizontally**, and **Rotate**. The Flip icons may be something you don't use too often with your overall image, but it's nice to know they are there when you need them. And the Rotate button is handy when you're bringing in a photograph that Luminar does not automatically rotate to the correct orientation (landscape vs. portrait). I do find that it is much easier to rotate the image—even without going into the Crop tool—by using the keyboard shortcuts `CMD` `[` and `CMD` `]` (PC: `CTRL` `[` and `CTRL` `]`).

- **Reset**: Click this button to reset all crop settings and start over.

ERASE

The Erase tool is great for removing elements in your image. I like to use Erase for sensor spots or facial blemishes, but you can also use it to remove people and other large objects from a photograph. The success and realism of the erasing effect is largely dependent on the photograph and how much you are trying to erase. Sometimes it works perfectly on the first try, but others you may need to work with it a few times before getting acceptable results.

This tool has a handful of options at the top:

- **Add**: This is the default setting you see soon after activating the Erase tool. Use this option to brush over areas that you want to erase. The brushed areas will be indicated by a red overlay.

- **Subtract**: If you accidentally paint over an area that you do not want to erase, select the Subtract option and then brush over the area to remove it.

- **Lasso (Mac only)**: If you have a large area that you want to erase but do not want to use brush strokes, then the Lasso might be a good option for you. This is best for areas with hard lines or sharp edges, such as buildings or other man-made objects, as it is a "connect-the-dots" type of lasso. Click around the area you want until you reach the beginning of your lasso, and a small circle will appear. Click this small circle to connect the lines and create a polygon.

- **Clear Selection**: Use this before clicking the Erase button when you want to clear all of your painted areas and start over.

- **Size**: This sets the size of the brush, and you can adjust it quickly by using keyboard shortcuts: **[** to decrease brush size and **]** to increase brush size.

- **Erase**: Click the Erase button when you are finished with the Paint and/or Lasso tools and want to erase the areas you have painted.

In the example below, I wanted to erase all of the distracting elements in the background of the image. First, I activated Erase at the top in the Tools drop-down menu. Next, I painted over the power lines and foliage until everything I wanted gone was painted with red. Finally, I clicked the **Erase** button; all of the distractions were removed from my image.

Before

Image with Erase brush strokes

After all elements were erased

CLONE & STAMP

The Clone & Stamp tool allows you to clone small areas of a photograph in order to *erase* or *copy* parts of the image. This is a good option when working with photographs with distinct patterns or man-made items.

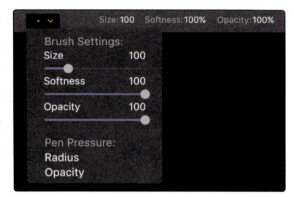

This tool has the standard brush settings at the top: **Size**, **Softness**, and **Opacity**. And if you use a pressure-sensitive tablet, such as a Wacom® Intuos®, you can use pen pressure adjustments as well.

To use this tool, first activate it from the **Canvas Tools** sidebar on the right. The first step after activating is to sample an area, which is the portion of the image you want to use as your initial copy. Once you see the small cursor with a cross hair in the middle of it, click over the area you wish to sample from. Then, the Brush tool will appear with a subtle translucent preview of the area you just sampled.

Sampling a section of the image

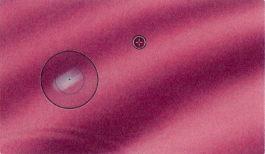
The translucent clone brush preview

LUMINAR 4: STEP BY STEP

CHAPTER 2: MASTERING YOUR WORKSPACE

The next step is simple: Brush across the area you wish to remove! If the area begins to look too "patterny" and shows obvious signs of cloning, then you might want to re-sample from another area. You can do this easily by pressing the **OPT** (PC: **ALT**) key and sampling from a new location.

Before cloning

After cloning

69

LENS & GEOMETRY

The last tool within the Canvas Tools group is Lens & Geometry. Here you can correct lens distortion, as well as chromatic aberration and lens vignetting. Below I've listed out each of the settings in this tool and how you can use them with your photographs.

One thing to keep in mind, however, is that this tool is only available on image layers. Also, some of the items within this tool differ depending on the type of image you are working on. For example, if you are editing a raw file, you will have all of the settings you see here. However, other image file types (PSD, JPEG, TIFF, etc.) will be missing a few of these settings.

- **Auto Distortion Corrections (raw only)**: With this setting, Luminar analyzes the image and also takes the camera and lens metadata into account to determine how to make this adjustment. The example below shows a photograph created with a very wide lens, which added some distortion in the scene, so I checked the Auto Distortion Corrections box to automatically fix it. Keep in mind that this setting also might *add* distortion to *other areas* of the image, particularly along the edges. So it's a good idea to really look at your photo closely when using this setting.

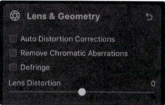

Before

After Auto Distortion Corrections

- **Remove Chromatic Aberrations (raw only):** Another setting within this panel is Remove Chromatic Aberration. Also referred to as "CA" or "purple fringing," chromatic aberration is an unwanted color distortion that can appear on the edges of items within a photo, usually in high-contrast areas. You might see this more often with lenses that are lower in quality; however, it can appear on high-quality lenses as well. Also, while this setting may not always *completely remove* the CA in a photo, it should allow you to *subdue* it. In the example below, I zoomed in to an area with a good amount of green-colored CA, and then I put a check in the **Chromatic Aberration** and **Defringe** boxes to help remove this color distortion.

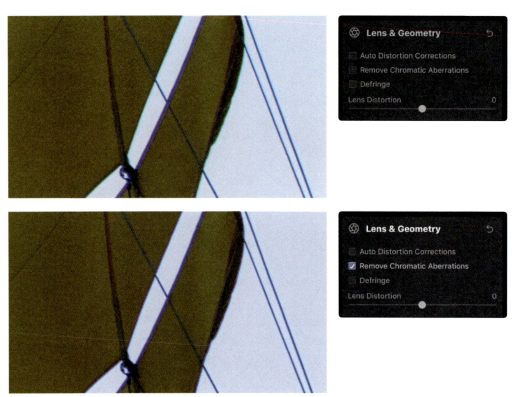

In this example, the top image shows some green CA along the right edge of the yellow object. Checking the Remove Chromatic Aberrations setting helps to remove this green discoloration.

- **Defringe**: Defringe is similar to removing chromatic aberrations, however it also applies to other types of halos. Sometimes this is a good option to use when the Remove Chromatic Aberrations setting does not remove all of the fringing in a photograph.

- **Lens Distortion**: The Lens Distortion slider helps to reduce barrel distortion. It can be used alone or in conjunction with the **Auto Distortion Corrections** setting. Moving the slider to the left gives the photo a more rounded/barrel shape, and moving it to the right will stretch the items on the edge of the frame. This is a good option to use when you have image distortion from a very wide-angle lens.

Lens Distortion: 0

Lens Distortion: –100

Lens Distortion: +100

These photos show what the image looks like at the extreme Lens Distortion settings (–100 through +100). In some cases you may find that there is a gray border around the final image. You will need to use the Crop & Rotate tool to remove this border.

- **Devignette**: Some lenses will add a vignette (darkened edges) to your photograph. If this is something you do not want in your image, then the Devignette slider is a good place to start. Move the slider to the right to lighten the edges of your image. This will likely be a very subtle correction.

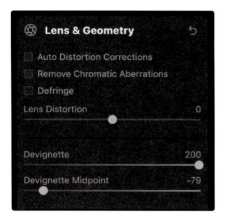

- **Devignette Midpoint**: This helps refine the Devignette setting. Move the Devignette Midpoint slider to the left to expand the correction area towards the center of the frame, and move it to the right to push it towards and off of the edges.

Devignette: 0
Devignette Midpoint: 0

Devignette: +200
Devignette Midpoint: 0

(Notice the white/lighter areas in the corners of the frame.)

Devignette: +200
Devignette Midpoint: −79

(The white/lighter areas are spread out towards the center of the frame.)

CHAPTER 2: MASTERING YOUR WORKSPACE

- **Transformation properties**: Lastly you have the ability to manually adjust the properties of the image to correct the distortion even further. This can be handy to correct for straight lines in a photo, such as with architecture photography. I find that making minor adjustments to these sliders can help to drastically improve the composition of an image. These sliders can also be used creatively, too! In the example below, I wanted to "pull" the plate of food closer to the front of the frame. So I first increased the Vertical slider, and then also increased the Scale to "crop" the excess gray area that was created from the previous slider adjustment.

Before

After

75

LOOKS

The Looks section in Luminar is where all of your pre-saved Looks are stored. When you first launch Luminar you will, by default, have a handful of Looks packs at your disposal. These Looks contain image adjustments that are saved, so you can easily add the same effects to one or more images. You can also import third-party Looks packs, as well as create and save your own! Plus, when you find some that you like and want to re-use, you can simply click the little star icon in the bottom-right corner of an individual Look to add it to the **Favorite Collection** for easy access on other images.

To access the Luminar Looks Collections, make sure that the Looks button is active in the toolbar at the top, and then click the **Luminar Looks** menu within the bottom filmstrip to view all packs.

CHAPTER 2: MASTERING YOUR WORKSPACE

IMPORTING A LOOKS PACK

Installing a third-party Looks pack is quite simple, but there's really only one method you should use to ensure everything gets installed properly:

nicolesy_sky_cloud_2.mplumpack

1. Download the Looks pack you wish to install (and be sure to unzip it if it ends with a *.zip* extension). You should have a file with a *.mplumpack* extension.

2. In the Luminar 4 menu bar, go to **File** > **Add Luminar Looks Collection**.

3. Navigate to your downloaded .mplumpack file. Select the file, and click Open.

77

4. Luminar will import the file and a small popup will appear when the pack is installed. Click OK. You will then be able to find this new pack inside of the Luminar Looks Collection window. ■

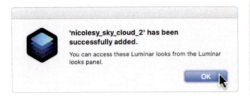

APPLYING A LOOK

Applying a Luminar Look is as simple as clicking on it inside of the Looks filmstrip at the bottom. Once you apply the Look, however, all *existing adjustments will be reset* and only the adjustments in the Look that was applied will affect your image. This is important to keep in mind, because you don't want to do a lot of work stylizing your image, only to discover that those settings disappear once you add a Look!

But there is a very simple workaround to make sure you have control over your editing workflow, and it includes working with Adjustment layers. Let's walk through this process so you can see how it works.

1. I started out with a raw file and made some basic edits to the tone and color, so nothing too dramatic. However I would like to use one of my existing Looks to add an overlay to the photo.

Before

After (raw adjustments)

2. Now I would like to apply one of my Looks, but I don't want the effects to overwrite any of the adjustments I have already applied. So I start out by activating the Layers panel.  Right now there is only one layer (the "base" layer), and all edits that have been added are applied to this layer.

3. Next, in the Layers panel, I click the ⊕ icon and select **Add New Adjustment Layer**. A new layer appears in the Layers panel.

4. Then, I choose a Looks pack that I want to work with (in this example, I will be using one of my paper overlays from the *Nicolesy ONE Hundred Vol. 2* pack). Because I am working on a new Adjustment layer, the overlay from the Look is applied to my photo without making changes to any of the existing edits. ■

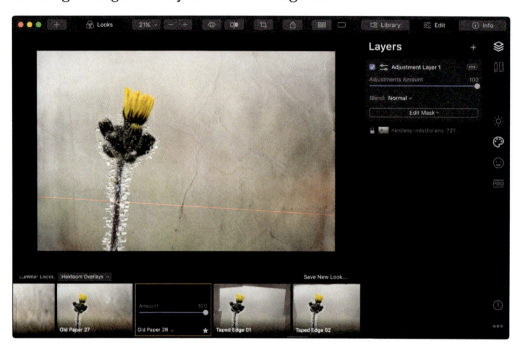

CREATING A CUSTOM LOOK

One last thing you may want to do is create your own Looks. Doing this is extremely simple! Once you've added all of the adjustments you want to save, click the **Save New Look** button . Give your new Look a name, and it will be saved to the User Luminar Looks collection. Also, keep in mind that only the adjustments *added to the current layer* will be saved in your Look.

EXPORT AND BATCH PROCESS

When working on files in Luminar 4, all edits are captured within the Luminar catalog. This means that your edits are saved as a working file, so long as the file remains within the catalog. However, when you want to save a finished version of the image (a JPEG, for example), then you will need to export the file.

EXPORTING TO IMAGE

When you are finished with your edits and ready to share or print your work, you will want to use the Export button located in the Top Toolbar, and choose **Export to Image**. This can also be accessed by going to **File** > **Export**. Doing this allows you to get the finished version of your image either on your computer or online via email, message, or social network.

- **Export to Image**: When exporting a file, most likely you will save the file as JPEG format, but you have the option to export it as a PNG, TIFF, PSD, and even PDF file as well.

  There are also some standard settings you can apply to your image as it is exported, such as **Sharpen**, **Resize**, **Color Space**, and **Quality**. I typically use this export option when saving the file as a JPEG to share either on my website or social media site, so the default settings are usually pretty close to what I want. The only thing I tend to change in the export window is the **Resize** drop-down menu. I rarely want to set this to Original (or Actual Size) when sharing online, so I will often set it to **Long Edge** and then change the pixel setting to **2000 px**. I also make sure that the **Quality** is set to **100** to ensure my image looks its best!

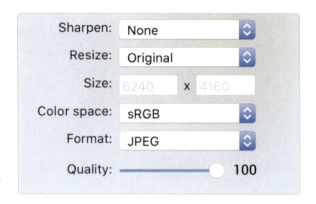

BATCH PROCESSING

Batch processing can be a very useful tool, particularly when you have multiple files that you would like to edit all at once. With batch processing, you can process and export multiple files in order to resize, rename, and add presets, all without having to open the files individually.

The Batch Processing feature can be accessed from a few different places. To access this feature, go to **File** > **Batch Processing** in the Luminar menu.

Next you will want to locate the images you would like to batch. The best way to do this is to have all of the images you want to work on already organized into folders and/or subfolders.

CHAPTER 2: MASTERING YOUR WORKSPACE

Note: If you are planning on creating a new preset to use on the images while batch processing, you will want to do it before the next step.

Now, access the Batch Processing window and browse for the folder of images you want to work on. You can also load the images by dragging the folder or images into the window. And, if you see any photos within the preview area that you do *not* want to include in the batch, hover over the image and click the small **X** that appears in the upper-left corner. When you are ready, click **Continue**.

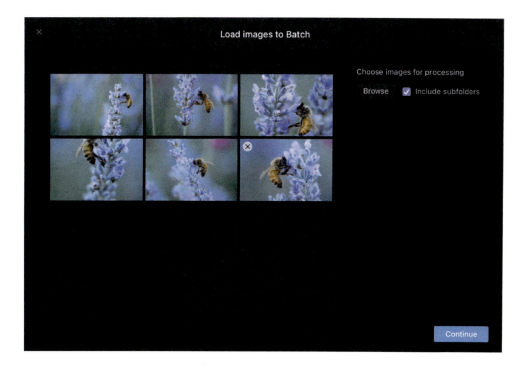

This next section is where you choose the settings for your batched files (see the "Batch Settings" image on next page). Think of it as another way to export images but with *extra options*. In the example above, I chose a Look I had created for these images, set a new location to save the processed files, changed the naming structure, and also resized the images to 2000 px wide.

83

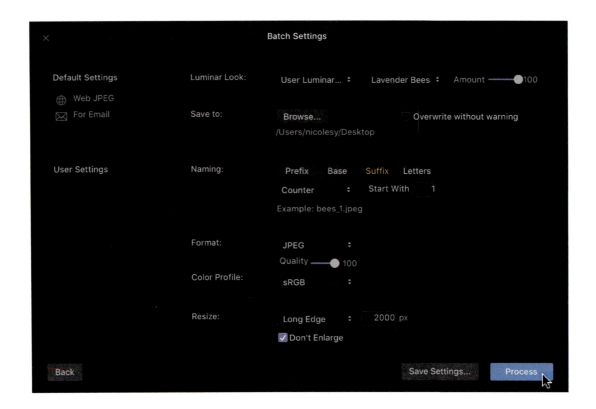

Once you have all of your options set, if you want to preserve the settings to use on other batch edits, click the **Save Settings** button on the bottom. When you're ready to process the photos, click the **Process** button on the bottom right. Luminar will batch process your group of images, and you will see the progress in a small pop-up window as Luminar goes through each photograph.

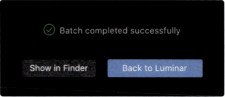

Once your images are processed, you can immediately view them in your folder to make sure they are to your satisfaction.

LUMINAR & PLUG-INS

One benefit of using Luminar is that you can use it in conjunction with other applications via plug-ins. In this section, I will explain how you can use the software from Lightroom Classic and Photoshop.

INSTALLING PLUG-INS

Before you get started, you first need to install the Luminar plug-ins into the appropriate applications. This is a very simple process that, for the most part, only requires a few steps. Here's how:

1. Go to the menu and select **Luminar 4 > Install Plugins** (Windows users, go to **File > Install Plugins**).

2. Click the **Install** button to the left of the program you wish to add the plug-in into. You may need to restart that software (such as Photoshop or Lightroom) in order for the plug-in options to appear in that software. ■

WORKING FROM LIGHTROOM CLASSIC

If you use Lightroom as your main raw processor and image organizer (also referred to as a DAM, or *Digital Asset Manager*), then you will likely want to use Luminar as a plug-in and continue editing the raw photos in Lightroom. Here's how to do this:

1. In Lightroom, process your raw photograph as you would like. In this example, I made some simple adjustments to the white balance and tone.

This is the edited file inside of Adobe Lightroom Classic.

LUMINAR 4: STEP BY STEP

CHAPTER 2: MASTERING YOUR WORKSPACE

2. Go to **File** > **Export with Preset** > **Edit a Copy with Lightroom Adjustments**. The image opens into Luminar where you can apply filters, Looks, layers, and other enhancements.

This option will apply any edits you made to the photo and bring it into Luminar, while the other option—Open Source Files—will bring your unedited raw photo into Luminar to edit the photo with no Lightroom adjustments applied.

3. After you have made all of your Luminar edits, click the **Apply** button on the top-left section of the window. Luminar closes, and the image appears alongside your original raw photograph in the Lightroom Library module. ∎

Once you apply your Luminar edits, the file will appear alongside the original inside of Lightroom. Here it is the TIFF file on the right.

87

WORKING FROM PHOTOSHOP

Another excellent option for using Luminar is from within Photoshop. This is a good option if you prefer to work in Photoshop when working on creative composites, such as detailed masking, design, or text edits, but would like to take advantage of Luminar's Tools and Looks to add a finishing touch. And, unlike working in Photoshop, you can easily make your Luminar file re-editable by using **Smart Objects**, as I will explain in the following steps.

1. In this example, I have a composite I created with layers and blending modes. I am finished with all of my Photoshop edits and would like to bring it into Luminar to add some stylization.

   To start, I first create a new stamped layer to merge all of the visible layers and create a new composite layer on top. So, I activate the top layer in the Layers panel and use the keyboard shortcut `CMD OPT SHIFT E` (PC: `CTRL ALT SHIFT E`), which adds a new layer to the top of my Layers panel.

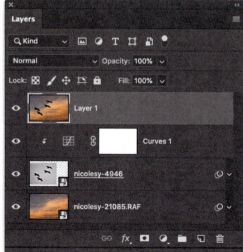

LUMINAR 4: STEP BY STEP

2. Now I can bring this photo into Luminar. But before doing that I would like to add one extra step. I prefer to keep all of my edits as re-editable as possible, and when using the Luminar plug-in in Photoshop you can easily do that by converting your layer into a **Smart Object**.

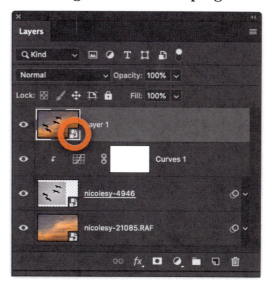

To do this, I make sure that the top layer is selected and then go to **Layer** > **Smart Objects** > **Convert to Smart Object**. A small icon appears in the bottom-right corner of the thumbnail in the Layers panel indicating that the photo is now a Smart Object.

3. Now I am ready to go into Luminar and make my edits. With the Smart Object layer still active, I go to **Filter** > **Skylum Software** > **Luminar 4**. Then, in Luminar, I add some Tools and effects. When I'm finished, I click Apply at the top-left area of the window.

4. Now, back in Photoshop, there is a new addition to the Layers panel: *Smart Filters*. This shows that I have made Luminar edits to the layer, and the best  part is that if I wanted to return to Luminar with that layer, all I would need to do is double-click the Luminar 4 text and the image would open up into Luminar with all of my previously-added filters (and other edits) still intact and editable. ◼

Chapter 3

ADJUSTMENT TOOLS

Post-processing tools in Luminar 4

One of the frustrations I hear most often with photographers using software with filters and presets, such as Luminar, is that they don't know where to begin. In this chapter, I will walk through all of the adjustment tools in Luminar 4 and explain how to best use each tool. This chapter does not illustrate every setting and slider within these adjustment tools, but rather a *small and refined selection* of settings that can have a big impact and be applied to a wide variety of images.

A cute little chipmunk • FUJIFILM X-T3, 60mm macro lens, 1/140 sec at f/2.4, ISO 160

ESSENTIALS

The Essentials adjustment tools will likely be your first stop for the majority of your photographic edits. Here you will be able to control the basic color, tones, sharpening, and other finishing touches.

LIGHT

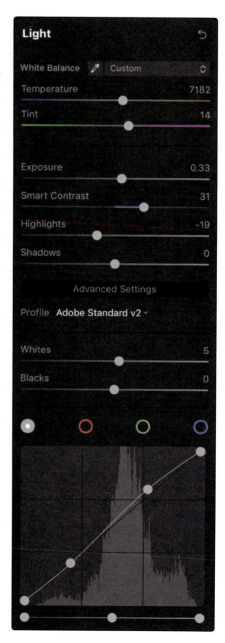

The Light tool is going to be the starting point for most photographs, particularly with raw images, but it is just as useful with other image file types as well. The Light panel is where you will adjust the white balance, tone, and contrast for your images. By default you'll see some basic adjustments, but if you click the Advanced Settings button it will open up to reveal even more settings, including the ability to choose a different camera profile.

When working with a raw file, you must use the Light panel adjustments on the main layer (not an Adjustment layer) to reap the full benefits of the raw capabilities. And, when working on non-raw image files, as well as Adjustment layers, you'll notice a few settings missing from the Light panel.

CHAPTER 3: ADJUSTMENT TOOLS

Most often, when I use the Light tool, I start with the **Temperature** and **Tint** sliders. I find it easier to first correct the color of my images, and then move on to the tonal adjustments. It's easier for me to see proper tone and contrast when the color is as balanced as possible, although this is purely a personal preference. Sometimes, I also will go back and forth between the white balance and tone adjustments to perfectly refine the Light settings in my photographs.

Before *After — Light*

In the example above, the color of the raw photo was very cool (many blue tones) and the Temperature needed to be increased. Making some slight increases to the **Temperature** and **Tint** sliders helped correct the color imbalance. I also changed the Profile to the *Adobe Standard v2* setting, mostly because I liked the way it looked better than the standard *Luminar Default* profile. Then, I played around with the tone adjustments to add a touch of brightness and contrast to the image. (All adjustments made to this photo are visible in the Light panel on the previous page.)

AI ENHANCE

One thing you'll find extremely useful in Luminar are the AI adjustment tools. With only a single slider you can make a huge visual impact on an image, and the AI Enhance tool is a combination of several adjustments in one. With the **AI Accent™** slider you'll likely notice a change to the tone and contrast of your photo, but there are also some subtle color enhancements as well.

Before

After — AI Enhance

CHAPTER 3: ADJUSTMENT TOOLS

And, if you have a photograph with a sky in it, using the **AI Sky Enhancer** will help boost the color and tones in the sky. The software is able to recognize skies (mostly blue skies) and performs corrections such as color, saturation, and even structural enhancements to clouds. And it also masks around any foreground objects to prevent the adjustments from affecting parts of the image that are not the sky.

AI STRUCTURE

Another useful AI tool is AI Structure. This tool has two sliders. The **Amount** slider determines the overall strength of the structure effect. Moving it to the *right* will intensify the details in your image, whereas moving it to the *left* will apply a

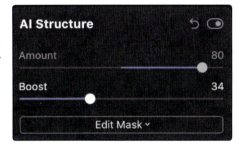

softening—and almost blurry—effect. The **Boost** slider will accentuate the details in your photo, giving the image an almost HDR look to it. One nice thing about this filter is that it is "human-aware" and tends to not over-process the skin and faces of people, giving them a much more natural look.

Before

After — AI Structure

95

COLOR

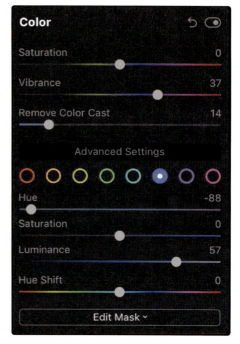

The Color adjustment allows you to manipulate the hue, saturation, vibrance, and luminance of colors in your image. You can adjust many of these settings either globally (across the entire image) or to specific color groups. There is also a **Remove Color Cast** slider that is very helpful when you can see that the color is "off" but can't quite fix it with the white balance settings within the Light panel. In fact, that small slider is probably one of my favorites in the entire application! It helps to clear away a "wash" of color in the image, such as a muddy or overly cool tone.

In the example below, I increase the **Vibrance** slider to give the entire image a nice boost of color. Then, in the **Advanced Settings**, I made some selective color edits to the **Greens** (intensifying the saturation and luminance of green stems of the tulips), as well as the **Blues** (altering the hue and luminance of the dog's shirt).

Before　　　　　　　　　　　　　*After — Color*

B&W CONVERSION

If you would like to convert your image to black and white, the B&W Conversion adjustment is the tool to use. Simple click the **Convert to B&W** button, and the image will turn to grayscale. Then, use the **Luminance** sliders to either brighten or darken areas in the image based on their colors.

For the strawberries, first I converted the image to black and white. Then I used the **Luminance** sliders to make the **Red** colors brighter and the **Cyan** and **Blue** colors darker.

Before

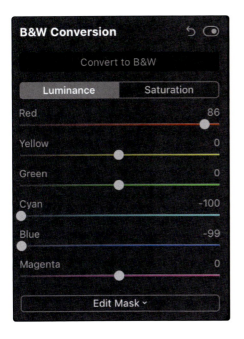

After — B&W Conversion

After — Luminance adjustments

Another option within the B&W Conversion adjustment is the ability to bring color back into the scene after making your initial black-and-white conversion. This allows you to create a scene where the majority of the photograph is black and white, but some color is still peeking through.

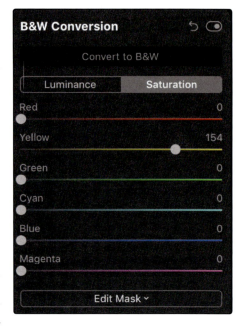

In the example below, first I converted the image to black and white. Then, I clicked **Saturation** to open that section, which revealed a group of similar-looking sliders. Instead of adjusting the brightness of the colors, however, these sliders saturate them to reveal all items in the image that contain that color group. So, I increased the **Yellow** slider to reveal all color within that color group, keeping the majority of the image in black and white with only the yellow showing.

Before

After — B&W Conversion with Saturation adjustments

DETAILS ENHANCER

The Details Enhancer adjustment will help you sharpen your photographs. There are a few things to keep in mind when sharpening a photograph. First, you can't sharpen something that is out of focus. If your image is blurry and has no point of focus, then no amount of sharpening will improve it. And second, this is one of those adjustments that you don't want to be too heavy-handed with. An over-sharpened photo is easy to spot and can start to look "crunchy" or grainy. Using a light touch is always the best approach when applying sharpening.

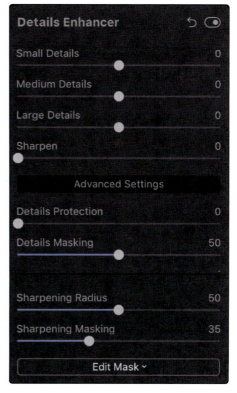

At a very basic level, sharpening is the process of adding contrast to the edges of elements within a photograph. Within Luminar there are several sharpening tools, and I'll go through a few of them here to help you understand what they can do with your photographs. This panel has a lot of sliders and can be a little bit confusing when you first start using it, but once you play with the sliders and really pay attention to your photograph, things will begin to become much more clear.

First, the most important thing you can do while sharpening your photographs is to zoom in to at least 100%. I tend to zoom in even further, typically to 200%. You also want to make sure that you are panning around the photograph and looking at all areas—both in-focus and out-of-focus—to make sure that you are sharpening only the parts of the image that you want to be sharpened.

Please note: In the example images in this section I've pushed many of the sliders well beyond what I would normally do while processing my own photographs. This is for demonstration purposes (sharpening differences are sometimes difficult to see in this environment) and also so that you can clearly see each effect in action.

- **Small, Medium, & Large Details:** These settings allow you to selectively control the small, medium, and large areas within your photograph.

Before

After — Small Details +100

After — Medium Details +100

After — Large Details +100

- **Sharpen**: This is the standard sharpening slider, which will help to de-focus the edges of all items in your image.

- **Details Protection**: When using the Details sliders, increasing this slider can help your photo to not look over-processed.

- **Details Masking**: This slider will mask out areas of the image so that you have more control over what is affected.

- **Sharpening Radius**: This setting will either increase or decrease the size of the sharpened edges. I like to think of this as an "intensity" adjustment.

Before

After — Sharpening +100 and Sharpening Radius +50

After — Sharpening +100 and Sharpening Radius +100

- **Sharpening Masking**: Adding masking to your sharpened image will help prevent large areas of solid color or out-of-focus regions from displaying any sharpened effects.

DENOISE

When you have a photo with a lot of noise or grain in it, the Denoise tool is very useful. The adjustment has three sliders: **Luminosity Denoise** removes grayscale (standard) noise, **Color Denoise** removes color noise, and **Boost** sets the aggressiveness of the noise reduction (think of it as an intensity slider).

In the example below, the image was photographed at ISO 12800, which introduced a lot of noise to the scene. By increasing the Denoise sliders I was able to remove most of the noise. However, moving them too far to the right can add a smudgy look, which is something you want to avoid. In fact, the example shows an excessive amount of noise reduction (far more than I would apply in any other setting), but for demonstration purposes an appropriate setting would be so subtle it would barely be visible in this book!

Before

After — Denoise

CHAPTER 3: ADJUSTMENT TOOLS

LANDSCAPE ENHANCER

The Landscape Enhancer works well on any outdoor image with green foliage. This adjustment has four sliders: **Dehaze** helps to cut through haze by adding contrast, **Golden Hour** adds a touch of warmth, softness, and glow to the scene, **Foliage Enhancer** boosts the colors of foliage and greenery, and **Foliage Hue** lets you adjust the color (moving the slider left makes green foliage warmer, and to the right makes it more green).

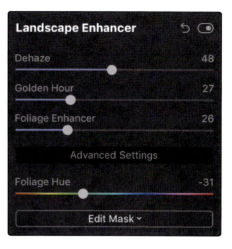

Before

After — Landscape Enhancer

103

VIGNETTE

A Vignette is a nice finishing touch to nearly all photos. Vignettes don't have to be intense; in fact, most of the time you probably won't even notice that a vignette was added to an image. However, they do help to subtly draw the eyes towards the main subject by darkening the edges of the image.

You can choose the type of vignette you want with the **Amount** slider (*left* for dark and *right* for light), and you can also adjust the **Size**, **Feather** (softness), **Roundness**, as well as add **Inner Light** to the center of the vignette. To change the position of the its center, click the **Choose Subject** button and click on your image (good for off-center subjects). And the **Mode** let's you tell Luminar if you want the vignette to appear on the edges of the original image (*Pre-crop*) or the cropped version (*Post-crop*). I recommend keeping this set to Post-crop for your images to ensure the vignette always appears on the edges of your photograph.

Before   *After — Vignette*

CREATIVE

The Creative group of adjustments allows you to have some fun with your photos! Add a texture overlay, drop in a new sky, colorize with a LUT file, give your scene some gorgeous sunrays, and more!

AI SKY REPLACEMENT

New to Luminar 4 is the AI Sky Replacement tool. This impressive adjustment lets you drop in a brand-new sky to your image, and then masks all of the foreground elements automatically! Although the default placement works well, additional settings allow you to fully customize the position and look of your sky replacement.

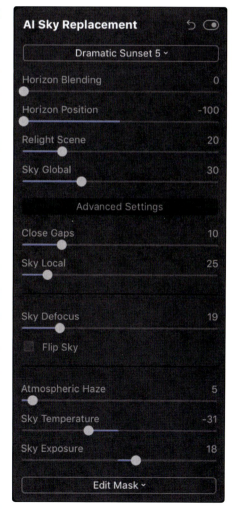

To use this tool, first choose a sky from the drop-down list. There are several built-in options to use, and you can also upload your own photo by selecting the **Load Custom Sky Image** option at the bottom of this list. When choosing a sky to use, it's best to stick with the existing light and time of day of your photograph. For example, you wouldn't want to place a sunset sky in an image that was photographed mid-day. You will also want to take note of the sun position as well. If the light was behind you and your subject was lit from the front when you photographed it, for example, you will want to avoid a sky image where you can see the sun behind the clouds.

- **Horizon Blending**: Think of this setting like a feather setting. Moving the slider to the right will increase the spread of the blend on the horizon. At a setting of 0 it still has a soft edge to it, but increasing the slider will make that edge even softer.

Before — Horizon Blending 0   *After — Horizon Blending +170*

- **Horizon Position**: This will move the position of the horizon (where the sky is blended) either up (move the slider to the right) or down (move the slider to the left). When adding a new sky, zoom in close to the horizon and analyze the blend to see if this setting needs to be adjusted.

Before — Horizon Position 0   *After — Horizon Position –14*

- **Relight Scene**: When you add a sky to an image, that new sky may have some color differences compared to the rest of the image. The AI Sky Replacement tool will light the scene (both tone and color) to help blend the original image with the new sky. In the example below, the mosque is quite blue, matching the morning light at the time it was photographed. But when I dropped in a new sky, by default the scene was re-lit to match the colors in that sky. I also increased the Relight Scene slider to intensify the effect.

Before *After — Relight Scene +60*

- **Sky Global**: This setting is similar to an opacity slider. Moving it to the right will make the new sky opaque and will cover up the existing sky. However, if you want the new sky to blend with your original sky, keep this slider at a lower setting.

- **Close Gaps**: This tool does a good job, but sometimes it leaves gaps in more detailed areas of a photo, such as between trees or branches. Use this slider to help fill in and close those gaps to reveal more of the sky overlay in your background.

Before — Close Gaps +10   *After — Close Gaps +26*

- **Sky Local**: If your original image's sky has existing clouds in it, this slider will help control the overlap of the old sky and new sky. If you see some of the original clouds in your photograph but want them covered up by the new sky, move this slider to the right until they disappear.

- **Sky Defocus**: When working with a photograph that has a blurry background, you'll want to make sure that you also blur the new sky so that it looks natural. Increase this slider to achieve this look.

Before — Sky Defocus 0   *After — Sky Defocus +78*

- **Flip Sky**: Flips the sky horizontally to help better with overall composition of your photograph.

- **Atmospheric Haze**: This setting adds haze to the sky, which helps blend a new sky more naturally with your photograph. In the example below, the sky I added was a bit too dark and intense, so I increased the slider to subdue the sky, allowing a better blend.

Before — Atmospheric Haze 0   *After — Atmospheric Haze +80*

- **Sky Temperature**: Use this slider when the sky is too cool or warm for your scene. In the example below, I wanted the light on the birds to be warmer, but the replacement sky was very cool. I increased the Sky Temperature slider, which then re-lit the overall scene to achieve the look I was seeking.

Before — Sky Temperature 0   *After — Sky Temperature +75*

- **Sky Exposure**: Lastly, you can adjust the exposure of the sky to better match your overall image. In the example below, the sky I added was too dark for my brightly-lit scene, so I increased the Sky Exposure slider to compensate for this difference.

Before — Sky Exposure 0

After — Sky Exposure +50

AI AUGMENTED SKY

Another fun addition to Luminar 4 is the AI Augmented Sky tool. This is similar to AI Sky Replacement, except it allows you to add individual objects into the scene, such as a moon, a rainbow, fireworks, birds, and so on. Luminar comes pre-installed with several objects you can use right away, however you are also able to add your own. To get started with this tool, first select an object using the **Object Selection** drop-down. Then you can work with the settings within the tool's panel to refine and reposition the object.

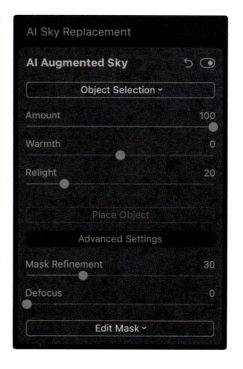

- **Object Selection:** Use this drop-down to select the object you would like to place into your image. If you want to add your own, choose the **Load Custom Image** option at the bottom. The best custom images to use with this option are going to be either transparent PNG files or a JPEG/PNG file with a solid black background. These files will not re-appear in this drop-down, so you will need to use this method each time you wish to place your own image.

- **Amount**: This sets the opacity of the object added to the sky. It is set to 100 by default, but you can reduce the slider to fade the effect and make it more transparent.

Before — Amount +100   *After — Amount +42*

- **Warmth**: Moving this slider to the left will make the object more cool (adding blue), and moving it to the right will make the colors of the object warmer (adding yellow/orange). Use this setting to help match the color of your existing sky.

Before — Warmth 0   *After — Warmth +45*

CHAPTER 3: ADJUSTMENT TOOLS

- **Relight**: The AI Augmented Sky tool will automatically try to match the colors and tone of the object to your original image. If you would like to change the intensity of the relighting effect, move this slider to the right. How the object changes may depend on what your original sky looks like, and I find with many of my photos that the object becomes less intense as I move the slider to a higher number. This works really well if your photo is hazy, as in the example below, but most often the default will be a good place to keep this setting.

Before — Relight +20

After — Relight +100

113

- **Place Object**: Click this button to give yourself the ability to move and resize the object within the image. The object will scale proportionally when resized from one of the corners, and you can also disproportionately stretch it by dragging along the side. The object can also be rotated as well (hover outside one of the corners until you see the cursor change into curved arrow). If you want to flip the object so it is showing in reverse (or is a mirrored version of itself), drag one edge in any direction until it goes beyond the farthest side.

  When you are finished with the transformation, either click the **Place Object** button again or press the **RETURN** or **ENTER** key on your keyboard.

Before Place Object *After Place Object*

- **Mask Refinement**: If you can see halos around the edges of your image, you may want to use this slider to help correct the masking. By moving this slider to the right, the masked edge will be shrunk closer to the subjects. When using this setting it's a good idea to zoom in so you can see the edge details up close. In the example below, I zoomed in to 300% so I could get a clear view of what was being affected.

Before — Mask Refinement +5   *After — Mask Refinement +80*

- **Defocus**: This slider will make the placed object blurry and out of focus, which is an essential step if your background is already out of focus.

Before — Defocus 0   *After — Defocus +80*

ADDING MORE THAN ONE OBJECT

One thing to keep in mind is that you can add this tool only once to a layer, so if you would like to add more objects to your sky—such as several individual clouds or a moon and some birds—you will need to add them on a separate layer.

First, make sure that all of the edits to your photo have been completed up to this point. This is particularly important if you are working with a raw photo and wish to make edits to the Light tool within the Essentials group of adjustments.

Once you have your photo ready with all edits applied up to this point, including the AI Augmented Sky, access the Layers panel. Then, click the ⊕ icon and select **Create New Stamped Layer.** *Now you are able to go back to the AI Augmented Sky tool where you can add another object to your sky.*

SUNRAYS

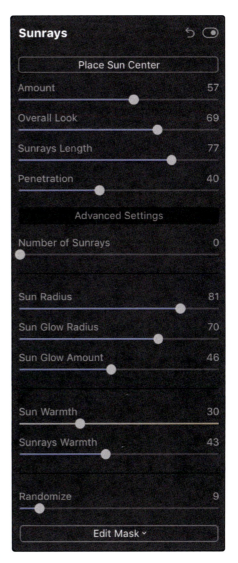

The Sunrays tool is a fun way to add beams of light to a photograph. To get started, first move the **Amount** slider to the right and you will begin to see the sunrays appear in your image. Then, click the **Place Sun Center** button and drag the white dot in your image. This is where the sunrays will originate from. I prefer to find an open spot of light to mimic the sun filtering from behind other image elements. In the example below, I set the rays to appear as though the sun is peeking through the trees above the waterfall. With this adjustment you want to make sure that the sun beams you are adding look as natural as possible. I tend to use this filter often on photographs I've taken in forests on overcast days, as the sun's direction is not so apparent when there are no harsh shadows in the scene.

Before

After — Sunrays

DRAMATIC

The Dramatic adjustment does two main things: It *decreases saturation* and *adds contrast*. It's a nice enhancement to photos that you want to look gritty or grungy, as a simple increase of the **Amount** slider will immediately give your image the desired effect. However, you can customize the look with some of the **Advanced Settings** as well.

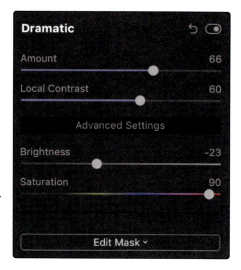

Before

After — Amount +66

After — Amount +66, Brightness –23

After — Amount +66, Brightness –23, Saturation +90

MATTE LOOK

The Matte Look adjustment is a stylistic effect that essentially reduces contrast and adds a haze over the image. It's a trendy look that can work on a wide variety of images. By increasing the **Amount** slider you will begin to see the effect: Black areas will become hazy and soft, and contrast will be reduced. In the **Advanced Settings** you can also add a color tone to the photo, which will be most noticeable in the blacks and shadow areas.

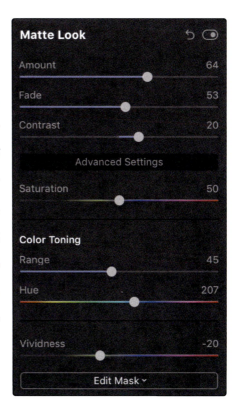

Before

After — Matte Look

MYSTICAL

The Mystical adjustment will add a glowing and ethereal look to your photos. I particularly enjoy using it on forest and waterfall photographs; it reminds me of a fairy-tale! But it can be used on a wide variety of images, as well. In the example below, the adjustment made the water brighter, and gave it a glowing look. I also increased the **Smoothness**, **Saturation**, and **Warmth** in the **Advanced Settings** to intensify the effect.

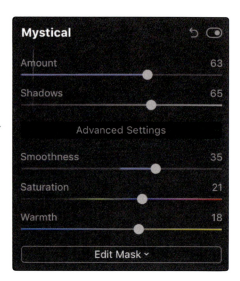

Before

After — Mystical

LUMINAR 4: STEP BY STEP

CHAPTER 3: ADJUSTMENT TOOLS

COLOR STYLES (LUT)

The Color Styles (LUT) tool allows you to colorize your photographs using Lookup Tables (LUT files). LUTs are essentially presets that contain both color and tonal data and can be used in many applications, which makes them very versatile. After applying the preset you can further customize the look by setting the **Amount**, **Contrast**, and **Saturation** of the added style.

Luminar 4 includes a good selection of default LUTs, and you can also load your own custom LUT file if you have some favorites you have downloaded or created.

Before

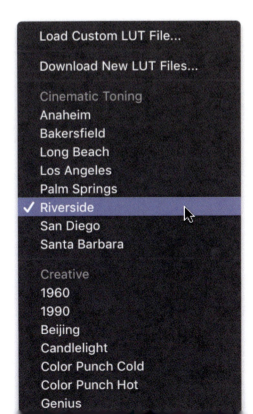

After — Color Styles (LUT)

121

TEXTURE OVERLAY

Using the Texture Overlay tool is a fun way to stylize a photograph. I like to use overlays to add light flares, old paper looks, and more.

To use this tool, first click the **Load Texture** button and choose an image file from your computer. Then you can flip the texture file to fit your composition, and also change the **Blend**, **Opacity**, and **Zoom** options. In the **Advanced Settings** options you can also adjust the color and tone of the texture file to better blend it with your image.

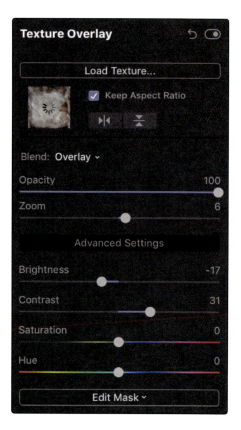

Before *After — Texture Overlay*

LUMINAR 4: STEP BY STEP

CHAPTER 3: ADJUSTMENT TOOLS

GLOW

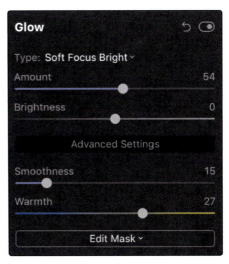

The Glow adjustment adds a bright glow to the light and white parts of an image, and is a good fit for photographs with water (waterfalls, crashing waves, etc.), or even portraits. Once you set the **Amount** slider you can also play around with the different **Type** settings. The default is *Soft Focus Bright*, which is a good option for most images when adding glow. But in some cases it might be a bit too powerful. Changing the Type—or playing around with some of the other sliders in this panel—will help you achieve the perfect glowy look.

Before

In this example, the Glow adjustment was perfect for this newborn portrait. Not only does it give a soft look to the image, it covers some of the redness and facial blemishes as well!

After — Glow

123

FILM GRAIN

The Film Grain adjustment in Luminar 4 is fairly straightforward: Increase the **Amount** slider to add grain. The **Advanced Settings** also have options for setting the tool's **Size** and **Roughness**.

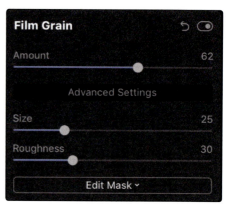

This is a good tool to use if you want to replicate an old-school film look by easily adding film grain. Another good use is when you are replacing a sky or doing any other type of composite work. Adding film grain to the photo helps make the image look more realistic and "blends" the layers together. All images have some noise in them, but when you put two different photographs together they don't always have the same quality and size of noise. Adding film grain helps to "disguise" the original noise and makes it appear as if all elements of the composite came from the same photograph.

Before

After — Film Grain

FOG

The Fog tool adds fog to the image, which is basically a wash of translucent white that ignores some of the darker areas of the scene. There are two **Type** options to choose from: *Light Fog* and *Dark Fog*. The

one you select will depend on your image, and I encourage you to play with them to view their differences on your images. I also find that this tool works well with masking, particularly the *Gradient mask*, which I've applied to the example below. In real-life fog, you can still see clearly directly in front of you, but visibility fades as you look farther away.

Before

After — Dark Fog with Gradient mask

PORTRAIT

If you photograph people then you will find the new portrait tools in Luminar 4 very useful. They work well but are not overpowering, allowing you to maintain a natural edit with your images.

AI SKIN ENHANCER

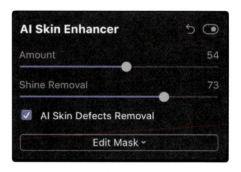

The AI Skin Enhancer tool focuses on skin by adding smoothing (**Amount**), removing shine (**Shine Removal**), and removing defects (**AI Skin Defects Removal**). One of the best things about it is that it works on photographs with multiple people, so it only takes one adjustment to affect the entire image. It also maintains a natural look by leaving small details alone, such as hair and eyelashes.

Before　　　　　　　　　　　　　　*After — AI Skin Enhancer*

AI PORTRAIT ENHANCER

If you want to add even more portrait adjustments beyond the AI Skin Enhancer, the AI Portrait Enhancer is a good fit. This tool let's you add **Face Light** (which helps draw the eyes towards their face), make adjustments to the eyes, eyebrows, lips, and teeth, and you can even slim the face and enlarge the eyes.

I highly recommend using a light touch with all of these adjustments. With most portraits the goal is to showcase the person at their best while still showing them as their true self. For example, a slight amount of face slimming and eye enlargement can improve a person's natural features, but adding too much pushes things into looking too unrealistic.

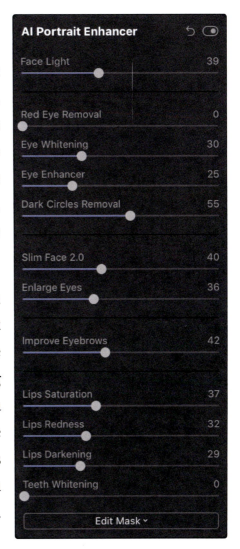

Before   *After — AI Portrait Enhancer*

HIGH KEY

A photograph that is "high key" means that it is bright with very little shadow detail, and oftentimes this term refers to something bright photographed against a light or white background (such as a white rose in the snow). In Luminar, the High Key adjustment tool tries to replicate that bright, overexposed look by adding a desaturated, bright, and somewhat washed-out effect. While this look works well for portraits, it can also be applied to other image types as well.

Before *After — High Key*

LUMINAR 4: STEP BY STEP

ORTON EFFECT

The Orton Effect tool is probably one of my favorites, and in fact it's one I've replicated manually in the past even before Luminar existed! You'll find it located here in the Portrait category, but this adjustment works well on nearly every single photograph. At its core, it adds saturation, contrast, and a slight glow effect, so while it works really well for portraits I also find that it looks great with landscapes, food, and so many other genres of images.

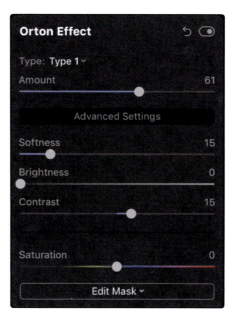

Before

After — Orton Effect

PROFESSIONAL

When you want more control when processing your photographs, the Professional category is the place to go. These tools are slightly advanced but still very approachable to new users.

ADVANCED CONTRAST

The Advanced Contrast tool lets you fine-tune the contrast in your image by targeting either the **Highlights**, **Midtones**, or **Shadows**. The **Contrast** sliders will increase the amount of contrast, and the **Balance** sliders change the balance of this contrast setting. Moving this setting to the right tends to make the targeted areas darker, whereas moving it to the left makes the targeted areas brighter.

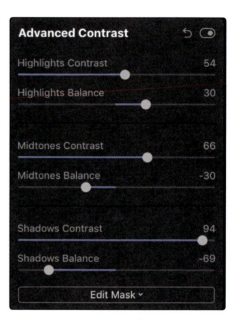

Before

After — Advanced Contrast

ADJUSTABLE GRADIENT

When you want to make selective edits to the top and bottom of your photo, you'll want to use the Adjustable Gradient tool. Here you can make both tone and color edits to either (or both) the top and bottom portions of the photo, allowing you to darken a sky, increase the color vibrance of the foreground, and so on. There is also a **Set Orientation** button, allowing you to reposition the "split" of the gradient.

Before   *After — Adjustable Gradient*

DODGE & BURN

The Dodge & Burn tool is an incredibly effective way to "sculpt" a photograph by painting in shadows and highlights. To begin adding this effect, first click the  **Start Painting** button and a new toolbar will appear at the top. Then, you can either paint to **Lighten** or **Darken** areas of the image. I recommend setting the brush's **Strength** setting to 10% so you don't over-process the image, and if you need more intensity, paint several brush strokes over the same area. And you can also reduce the **Overall Amount** after you've made your edits, just in case the result is overpowering.

Another good rule of thumb when painting is to use the *Lighten* brush on areas that are already bright, and use the *Darken* brush on areas that are already dark. This will allow you to fully control the amount of contrast and intensity you are adding to your photo. You can also use this tool to create a custom vignette as well by darkening the edges.

Before　　　　　　　　　　　　　　*After — Dodge & Burn*

COLOR ENHANCER

When you want to add even more color edits to your photo, the Color Enhancer tool gives you a *lot* of options! Here you can edit the **Brilliance** (which is similar to a saturation adjustment), **Warmth**, and you can also add **Color Contrast**, which helps create tonal contrast between colors opposite each other on the color spectrum.

Another fun setting is **Split Color Warmth**, which lets you selectively adjust the color temperature of the warm and cool areas. And **Color Balance** at the bottom allows you to create your own customized split-toned or cross-processed effect, specifically targeting the **Shadows**, **Midtones**, and **Highlights**, to alter and enhance their color values.

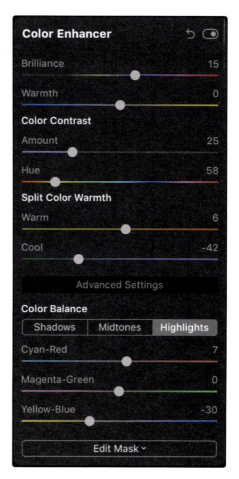

Before

After — Color Enhancer

PHOTO FILTER

The Photo Filter tool mimics what an actual colorized photo filter would do if you added one to your lens when creating your image. Oftentimes you will use this type of filter to add a warm (yellow/orange) or cool (blue) effect, but in Luminar you can select any color you desire. This adjustment can be used to

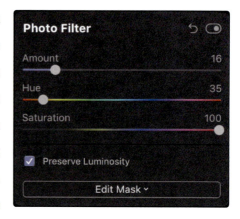

stylize a photo, or to correct for a color-cast that you can't remove using other methods.

The settings in this tool are fairly straightforward: **Amount** sets the intensity of the effect, **Hue** allows you to select the color, and **Saturation** lets you decrease the saturation of the color chosen in the Hue slider. Also, the **Preserve Luminosity** checkbox is checked by default, which is going to be ideal for most images. It prevents the color from the Photo Filter tool from affecting the tones in the image, so that it is only altering the colors.

Before

After — Photo Filter

SPLIT TONING

Last in this list is Split Toning, a great way to give your image a cross-processed or colorized effect. You can go as subtle or extreme as you like with this tool, and it can also give your photo an old-school film look as well.

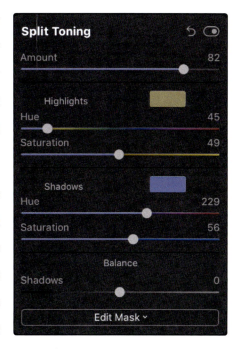

To get started, you'll first want to increase one of the **Saturation** sliders. This will allow you to see the effect start to take hold. Then, adjust the **Hue**, which allows you to choose the color. The **Highlights** and **Shadows** sections will target the above two adjustments to those tonal regions, and the **Balance** slider at the bottom of the panel lets you shift which color is more prominent. I tend to prefer a yellow/blue split toning effect with my images, adding a classic colorized effect that works on many types of photographs.

Before *After — Split Toning*

Chapter 4

HONEY BEE

A clean and colorful edit

One of my favorite subjects is bees. Photographing them is tricky, as they move very quickly and getting them in focus is a challenge, but when I get one just right the results are fantastic. Plus, because they are oftentimes photographed surrounded by flowers, it almost always makes for a colorful result.

To get started with this walkthrough, access the image listed below and open the photo in the **Edit** view inside of Luminar 4.

Image used with this chapter: *nicolesy_honey_bee.RAF*

A bee on a lavender flower • FUJIFILM X-T3, 60mm macro lens, 1/1000 sec at f/3.2, ISO 1250

STEP 1

The very first thing this photo needs is some help with composition. The bee and flower are very small in the scene, and cropping it will help make the subject more prominent.

To do this, I select the Crop tool in the toolbar at the top. I keep all settings unchanged to ensure the image's aspect ratio remains the same, and then I drag from each corner to crop the image to set the crop. I also want to make sure that the bee is situated on the top-right third-line of the frame, which results in a pleasing composition.

CHAPTER 4: HONEY BEE

STEP 2

The next step is to adjust the color. Because this is a raw file there is a lot of data in the image file that can be "pulled out" and brought back to its true values.

In the *Essentials* category, I first go to the **Light** tool. Then, I click **Advanced Settings** to open up more options, and in the **Profile** drop-down menu I select the **Adobe Standard v2** option. This is a subtle change, but I like the colors in this profile versus the Luminar Default profile.

139

STEP 3

Still in the Light tool, I go to the very top to adjust the White Balance sliders. Out of camera this image is too blue and does not reflect the true colors of the scene. So, I make the following adjustments to add warmth to the photograph:

- **Temperature +8473**
- **Tint +20**

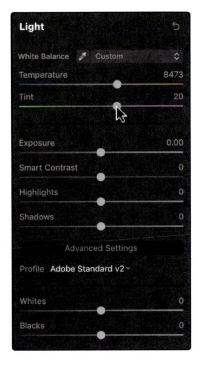

STEP 4

Next, I would like to add some contrast to the image. It looks a little flat, and the quickest way to do this is with a curve.

So, I go to the bottom of the **Advanced Settings** within the Light tool, click the upper-right intersection of the graph, and drag it up to add brightness to the image. Then, I click the lower-left intersection of the graph and drag it down, which adds darkness and contrast. This curve shape is called an S-Curve and is a very common way to add contrast to a photograph.

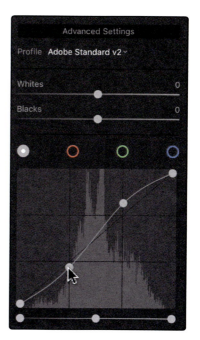

STEP 5

I'd like to make a few more adjustments within the Light section to fine-tune the tones and bring out some of the details in the highlights and shadows. So, I make the following adjustments:

- **Highlights −28**
- **Shadows +32**
- **Whites +12**

STEP 6

I access the AI Enhance tool next. This tool does a great job of adding a boost of color and contrast to a photo with only one simple

slider. I increase the **AI Accent**™ to **+30**, which adds a nice subtle change to the Photo. It might not be visible in the example above, but you will see it in your own edits!

STEP 7

One thing I noticed is that the lavender is quite light and could use a boost. So, still in the *Essentials* category, I access the Color tool. I click **Advanced Settings** to expand the panel, and this is where I am able to selectively adjust color groups in a photo. I first click the Purple color group, and then increase the **Saturation** to +50 while also decreasing the **Luminance** to −53 in order to make the lavender darker and more colorful.

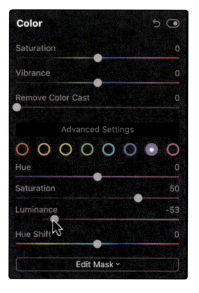

STEP 8

Even though this photo is sharp and in focus, I'd like to add a bit more sharpening, but only to the already-in-focus areas. I zoom in to **200%** to see the image up close, and then I access the Details Enhancer tool and set the **Sharpen** slider to *+55*.

However, I don't want the sharpening to affect the out-of-focus areas, so I click **Advanced Settings** and increase the **Sharpening Masking** slider to *+67*. This auto-masks the sharpening effect so it applies to the appropriate areas only.

STEP 9

Next, I head over to the *Creative* category and access the Mystical tool. This tool helps add a touch of glow and saturation to a photo, which is perfect for this colorful bee image.

I adjust the **Amount** slider to **+43** to show the effect, and then I access the **Advanced Settings** and increase the **Saturation** to **+25**, which helps boost the color.

STEP 10

I'd like to make a few more adjustments to the color, so I head over to the *Professional* category and select the Color Enhancer tool. I first increase the **Color Contrast Amount** to **+13**. This intensifies the contrast in the bee by making it brighter, and also adds a slight amount of contrast to the background.

Then, I go to the **Split Color Warmth** section and set the **Warm** slider to +5 and the **Cool** slider to –16, which enhances both the warm and cool colors in the photo.

STEP 11

Lastly, I finish up by going back to the *Essentials* category and adding a Vignette. I set the **Amount** to **−64** to darken the edges, then I click the **Advanced Settings** button to reveal more options. Here I set the **Roundness** to **+20** and **Feather** to **+22**, which makes the vignette more circular and softer. I also add a touch of **Inner Light**, and set it to **+10**, making the center of the image brighter, helping to direct the viewer's eyes towards the center of the frame. ◼

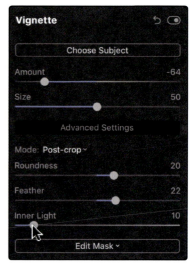

CHAPTER 4: HONEY BEE

Before

After

149

Chapter 5

ROCKY COAST

Bringing life to a gloomy sky

I love the Oregon coast, and it's a perfect playground for photographers. Although there are a lot of gorgeous rocky formations to find and photograph, the weather does not always cooperate. An overcast day can be perfect lighting for certain aspects of the scene, but sometimes it's nice to have a few clouds in the sky, too. In this chapter, I will take a nice photo of the coast and give it some life with some clouds and coloring.

Images used with this chapter:
nicolesy_rocky_coast.RAF
nicolesy_rocky_coast_sky.JPG

The Oregon Coast • FUJIFILM X-T3, 18–55mm lens, 0.6 sec at f/11, ISO 200

STEP 1

For this photo, the very first thing I'd like to do is add a new sky. I'm doing this first because I want to make sure that all of my other edits mesh well with the sky addition.

So, I open the image into the **Edit** view, and then go into the *Creative* category where I activate the AI Sky Replacement tool. I also click the **Advanced Settings** button to reveal all of the options in this set of adjustments.

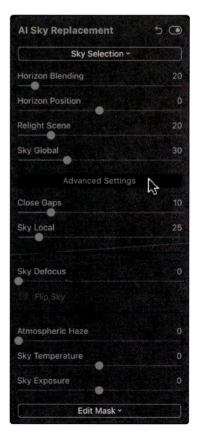

STEP 2

Next, I click the **Sky Selection** drop-down menu and, at the very bottom, choose **Load Custom Sky Image**. Then I access the *nicolesy_rocky_coast_sky.jpg* file, and click **Open**. This adds the new sky to my photo, but it still needs some work to make it blend better with this scene.

(I'm not concerned with the reflection in this particular scene, so I won't be adding the sky to the water. There are a lot of ripples and the color will match when the sky edit is complete, so I can get away with it as-is.)

STEP 3

The first slider I adjust is **Horizon Position**. I set this to **−41**, which reveals a different part of the clouds in the sky.

I also notice that some of the sky did not fully cover the background on the left portion of the frame. To fix this, I go down to the **Sky Local** setting and increase it to **+44**, which is just enough to fill in that empty space.

STEP 4

Now I want to adjust the look of the sky itself. At the bottom of the panel, I increase the **Atmospheric Haze** setting to **+72**. There is a touch of haze in the photo already, so this helps to neutralize it and make it mesh better with the foreground.

I also decrease the **Sky Temperature** all the way to **–100**, which balances the color of the sky better with the image.

STEP 5

Now I need to go back to the *Essentials* category and make some adjustments using the Light tool. The image is very cool, and I'd like to add a touch of warmth. So, I increase the **Temperature** slider to **8726**, which cuts out some of the overpowering blue colors.

STEP 6

Still in the Light tool, I go down to the tonal adjustments. First I increase **Smart Contrast** to **+28**, which adds a nice touch of contrast to start off. This adjustment adds some darkness to the rocks, so I also increase the **Shadows** to **+24**, which brings back some of the detail in the rocks and sand area while still maintaining some of the contrast from the previous adjustment.

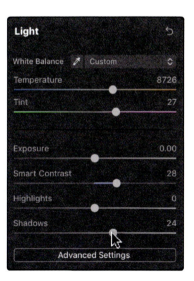

STEP 7

I'd like to see a bit more contrast in the image, so in the Light tool I click the **Advanced Settings** button to reveal more settings. Then, in the **Tone Curve**, I click the upper-right intersection of the graph and drag up to add brightness to the image. I then click the lower-left intersection of the graph and drag down, creating an S-Curve which adds darkness and contrast.

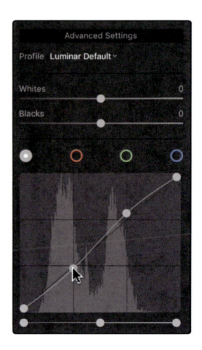

LUMINAR 4: STEP BY STEP

STEP 8

Next, I move my attention to the AI Structure tool. This image has a lot of rough rocks, and adding some structure can help make them really pop. So, I increase the **Amount** to **+20** and the **Boost** to **+12**, which intensifies the texture in the rocks.

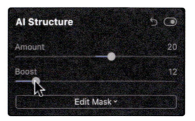

STEP 9

When processing landscapes one of my favorite tools to use is the Mystical adjustment, located in the *Creative* category. I set the **Amount** to +29, which adds a touch of contrast and subtle glow to the photograph.

CHAPTER 5: ROCKY COAST

Before *After Film Grain (200% zoom)*

STEP 10

Still in the *Creative* category, the next step is to use the Film Grain tool, which will help blend together the newly-added sky and the main image, making them look cohesive. To enhance the illusion that they were photographed at the same time, I set the **Amount** to **+10** which adds a touch of grain to the entire photograph.

It's a subtle change, so you may need to zoom in to 100% (or more) to see the difference.

161

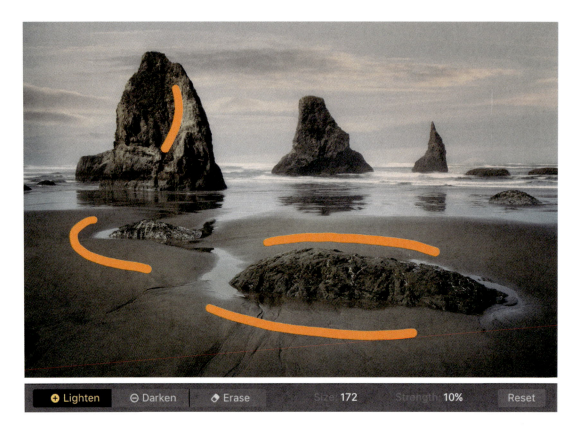

STEP 11

The next thing I'd like to do is add some custom dodging and burning to "sculpt" the light in the scene. I start by accessing the Dodge & Burn tool in the *Professional* category, and click the **Start Painting** button.

Then, in the toolbar at the top, I keep the setting at **Lighten**, but change the **Strength** to **10**%. Then, with the **Brush Size** set to **172**, I make several brush strokes on the sand and the large rock, trying to focus the brush strokes on areas that are already light.

CHAPTER 5: ROCKY COAST

STEP 12

Next, in the toolbar, I change the setting to **Darken** and again set the **Strength** to **10%**. Using the **Brush Size** set to **100**, I paint over some of the darker areas in the photo, particularly the rocks.

Adding this adjustment (including the Lighten painting from the previous step) helps to add a customized type of contrast to the photo.

STEP 13

One thing I like to do is stylize my photos with the Color Styles (LUT) filter in the *Creative* category. Using the drop-down menu, I set the LUT style to **1960**. Because this particular LUT file adds some fade to the photo, I also increase the **Contrast** to **+20** to bring back the original contrast in the photo.

CHAPTER 5: ROCKY COAST

STEP 14

I head back over to the *Essentials* category and focus my attention on the Landscape Enhancer tool. This scene still has quite a bit of haze to it, so I increase the **Dehaze** slider to **+26**. This does a very good job of bringing out the color in the sky and also making the rest of the photo look a little more clear.

STEP 15

For the final step, I go down to the Vignette tool to darken the edges and give the photo a nice finish. I make the following adjustments to this tool to help draw the eyes more towards the center of the frame:

- Amount −48
- Size +60
- Roundness +13
- Feather +29
- Inner Light +5

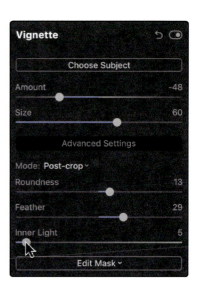

CHAPTER 5: ROCKY COAST

Before

After

167

Chapter 6

MOSSY FOREST

Processing a smartphone photograph

Sometimes I like to go on short adventures and leave the camera behind. The best part about our technology now is that we can still always have a camera with us if we choose to in the form of a mobile phone! I have my iPhone handy at all times, so while hiking one day I decided to leave my camera at home. But it didn't stop me from creating photographs! The forest was beautiful that day, and I even managed to get a few keepers.

Image used with this chapter: *nicolesy_mossy_forest.DNG*

A mossy forest in Oregon • iPhone 11 Pro, 1/120 sec at f/2.0, ISO 40

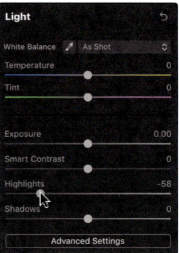

STEP 1

For the most part the tones in this image are not bad. It's a little flat, but I don't want to overwhelm the image by adding too much contrast because I will be adding quite a bit of stylization in later steps that might overpower it. However, I would like to subdue the very bright whites in the top-right corner of the frame. So, starting in the *Essentials* category, I use the Light tool and reduce the **Highlights** to −58. I'll be adding a sunray to this area in a later step, so I don't mind that it's still a little bit washed out (even after this adjustment).

Before *After Color correction (200% zoom)*

STEP 2

Another thing I notice in that same upper-right area of the frame is that there is quite a bit of fringing (the blue/purple highlights on the edge of the branches). I could try using the Lens Correction tool, but I suspect that this will need more of a manual correction.

So, I go down to the Color tool and click the **Advanced Settings** button. Then, I access both the **Blue** and **Purple** color toggles and reduce their **Saturation** sliders to **−60**. This removes the blue/purple fringing along the edges of the trees, and because there are no other blue or purple colors in the photo it won't affect anything else.

171

STEP 3

Next I would like to add the sunray to this photo, so I go over to the *Creative* category and access the Sunrays tool. The bright area in the top-right corner—and the fact that the light is diffused so there's no obvious sun direction—makes this a great candidate. I begin by increasing the **Amount** to **+66**, which makes the adjustment visible. Then, I click the **Place Sun Center** button and drag the sunray to the bright area in the corner of the frame. I also increase the **Sunrays Length** slider to **+73** to lengthen the beams. I click **Done** at the top to commit the change.

STEP 4

I next click the **Advanced Settings** button to customize the look of the sunrays. First, I decrease the **Number of Sunrays** slider to +14, which makes the sun beams a bit softer.

I also go down to the **Randomize** slider at the very bottom and watch my image while I move the slider until I find a setting that looks good. For this example I set it to +28, however you may find a different look more suited to your preferences.

STEP 5

Now that I've added the sunrays, I'd like to go back to the *Essentials* category to make a few more basic adjustments. I start with the AI Enhance tool and increase the **AI Accent**™ slider to **+36**. This gives the image a boost of tone and contrast without being overpowering.

STEP 6

Still in the *Essentials* category, I go down to the Landscape Enhancer. With all the greens in this photo it is a perfect candidate for this tool!

I start by increasing the **Dehaze** slider to +27, which helps cut through some of the haze by adding contrast. Then, I increase the **Golden Hour** slider to +7 to add a touch of warmth. Lastly, I increase the **Foliage Enhancer** to +14 to boost the brightness and saturation in the moss and ferns. But be careful with this slider! Too much to the right, and the greens can begin to look unrealistic.

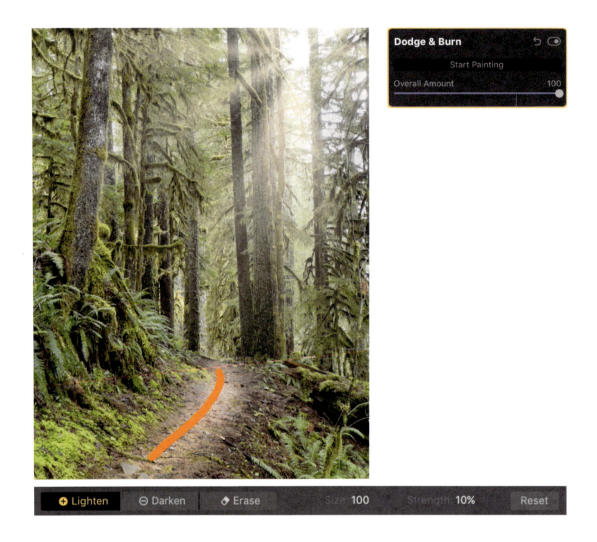

STEP 7

Next, I head over to the *Professional* category and activate the Dodge & Burn tool. I click the **Start Painting** button and go to the toolbar at the top where I make sure that the mode is set to **Lighten** and the **Strength** is set to **10%**. Then, with a **Brush Size** of **100**, I begin brushing along the center of the path near the bottom of the screen. This lightens the path and makes it much more apparent.

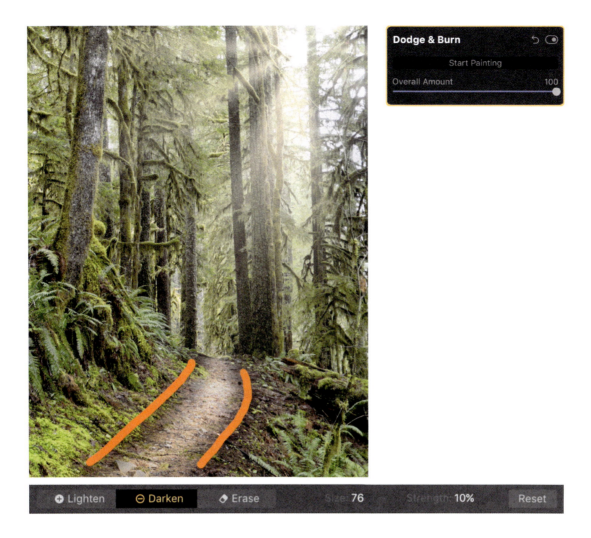

STEP 8

Still in the Dodge & Burn tool, I change the mode to **Darken** and again make sure that the **Strength** is set to **10%**. I also decrease the **Brush Size** to **76**, and this time I paint along the edges of the path. This adds contrast to the adjustment and really makes the brighter path area stand out.

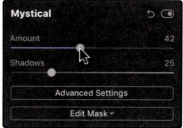

STEP 9

Another wonderful tool to use for a beautiful, mossy landscape scene is the Mystical tool, located in the *Creative* category. To apply this adjustment, I simply increase the **Amount** slider to **+42**. This adds a beautiful, glowing, fairy-like feel to the image.

STEP 10

Still in the *Creative* category, I go to the Color Styles (LUT) tool to add a touch of color change to the image. In the drop-down menu I select the **Anaheim** LUT style and leave all other settings as-is. This intensifies the green glow of the scene without altering the colors too much.

STEP 11

Lastly, I go back to the *Essentials* category and access the Vignette tool. I keep this adjustment simple—and subtle—by changing only the **Amount** slider, which I set to **−50**. This adds a touch of darkness to the edges, creating a nice finishing touch to this fairy-like forest scene. ■

CHAPTER 6: MOSSY FOREST

Before

After

181

Chapter 7

COOLING TOWER

Adding a new sky with style

Sometimes it's fun to take a seemingly bland photo and give it life. This photo is of a cooling tower of an abandoned and never-completed power plant in Washington, USA. While the subject itself is quite interesting, the sky left something to be desired. A new sky and some color and tone adjustments help to give this photo a new look.

Image used with this chapter: *nicolesy_cooling_tower.DNG*

The Satsop cooling tower in Washington, USA • FUJIFILM X-T1, 12mm lens, 1/500 sec at f/11, ISO 200

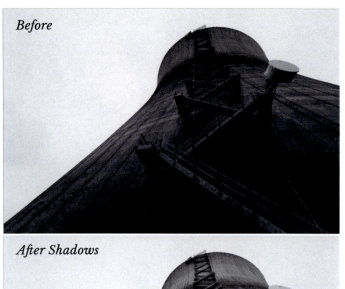
Before

After Shadows

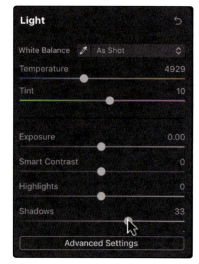

STEP 1

The tower in this photo is quite dark, so I would like to add brightness to make the details more clear. I begin in the *Essentials* category with the Light tool. I increase the **Shadows** slider to **+33** to make the tower much more visible.

STEP 2

Next, I go down to the AI Structure tool and set the **Amount** to **+22**. There is a lot of texture in the building, and I'd like it to look more pronounced. This setting is a good amount without making it look too "crunchy" or over processed.

STEP 3

Now it's time to add a brand-new sky, so I head over to the *Creative* category and access the AI Sky Replacement tool. Then, from the **Sky Selection** drop-down menu I choose the **Sunset 1** sky to give the background a whole new look. I also increase the **Relight Scene** setting to **+100** to help prevent the halo that was surrounding the tower after the new sky addition. The image looks very dark now, but that will be fixed in later steps.

CHAPTER 7: COOLING TOWER

STEP 4

Still in the AI Sky Replacement tool, I click the **Advanced Settings** button to display more options. Here I make the following adjustments to help blend the sky better with the environment by adding haze, adding the warmth to the sunset, as well as increasing the sky's exposure:

- **Atmospheric Haze +30**
- **Sky Temperature +40**
- **Sky Exposure +40**

STEP 5

I'd like to continue editing this photo, but I want to make sure that the edits I make are applied to the entire image (including the sky), and not only the cooling tower.

To do so, I click the Layers Panel icon in the right toolbar, then I click the ⊕ icon and select **Add New Adjustment Layer**. Now any edits I make on this Adjustment layer will apply to the overall image.

  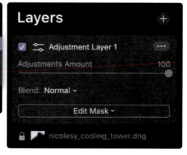

STEP 6

With the new Adjustment layer active, I access the *Essentials* category and select the Light tool. Some of the adjustments in previous steps made the image look too dark, so I make the following settings to increase the brightness and contrast:

- **Exposure +0.72**
- **Smart Contrast +30**
- **Shadows +20**

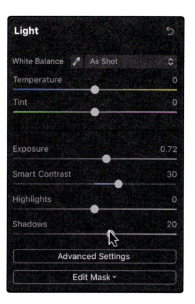

STEP 7

Still in the *Essentials* category, I go down to the Color tool. Here I increase the **Remove Color Cast** setting to **+83**. This helps balance out the colors in the image by removing some of the yellow tones from the tower and also adds a subtle touch of tonal changes as well.

CHAPTER 7: COOLING TOWER

STEP 8

Next, I head over to the *Creative* category and access the Color Styles (LUT) tool. Then, I select the **Wooden** LUT file from the drop-down menu to give the image a slight creative color style.

STEP 9

I'd like to add even more stylization to this, so I go up to the Matte Look tool. I increase the **Amount** slider to **+40** to add the matte effect, and I increase the **Fade** slider to **+36** to intensify this look. The result from this adjustment gives the photo somewhat of an aged feel to it.

Before / *After Film Grain (300% zoom)*

STEP 10

Because I added a new sky to this photo, one thing I'd like to do is also add some film grain, which will help make the sky and original image blend together more cohesively. If you look at the image above you can see in the "Before" photo that there is grain in the sky, but not in the tower. This step will help balance that out.

I go down to the Film Grain tool and increase the **Amount** to +**22**. I also click the **Advanced Settings** button and reduce the **Size** to +**5** and the **Roughness** to +**10** to make the grain less prominent.

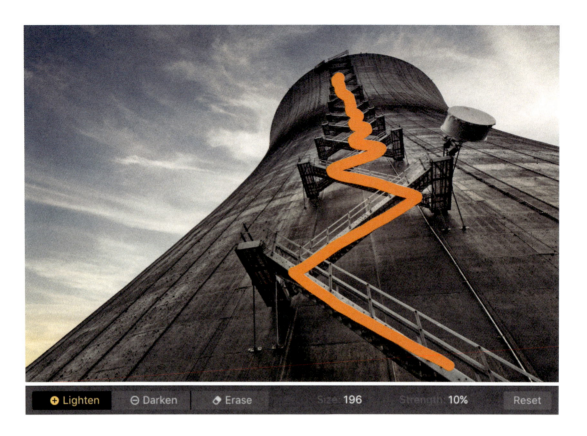

STEP 11

Next, I would like to make some custom light enhancements using dodging and burning. I go to the *Professional* category on the right, access the Dodge & Burn tool, and click **Start Painting**.

In the toolbar at the top I make sure that **Lighten** is selected, reduce the **Strength** setting to **10%**, and also increase the brush's **Size** to **196**. Then, I brush over the zigzag of stairs to intensify their brightness.